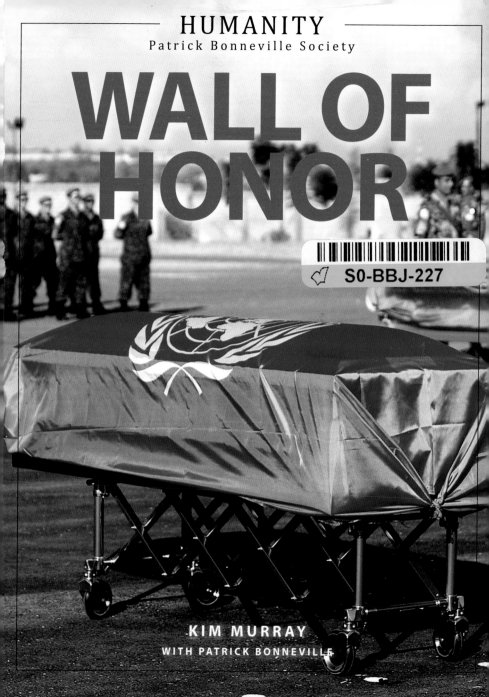

# HUMANITY
## Patrick Bonneville Society

# WALL OF HONOR

S0-BBJ-227

**KIM MURRAY**

WITH PATRICK BONNEVILLE

# HUMANITY
## Patrick Bonneville Society

# WALL OF HONOR

**100 ORGANIZATIONS
KEEPING THE WORLD TOGETHER**

**DESIGNED BY
PATRICK BONNEVILLE**

This book is dedicated to all Red Cross and Red Crescent workers and volunteers from all over the world. You are an inspiration. Thank you, Mr. Dunant, for your vision.

Patrick Bonneville

The publisher offers special thanks to Kim Murray, Shannon Partridge, Kelli Ann Ferrigan, Gina Garza, Lori Baird Isabelle Paradis and Philippe Hemono. The publisher also offers thanks to Céline Laprise, Caroline Leclerc and Louis Dubé from the SODEC. *Merci à tous.*



First edition

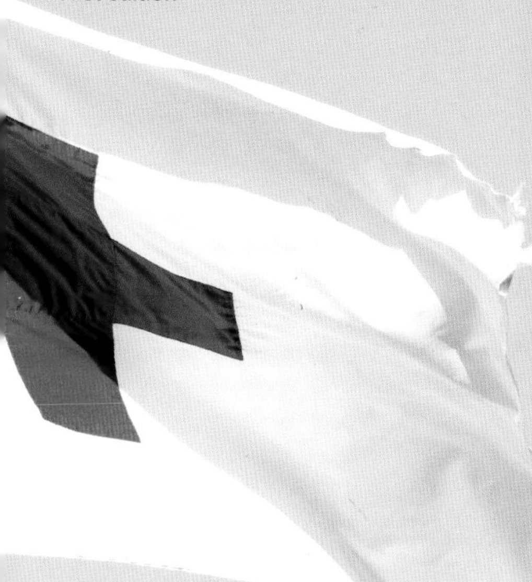

Published by
PATRICK BONNEVILLE SOCIETY
310 Parmenter, Sutton, Quebec
J0E 2K0 Canada
www.patrickbonneville.ca

**Writer:** Kim Murray
**Research:** Kim Murray, Patrick Bonneville
**Editor:** Shannon Partridge
**Proofreading:** Kelli Ann Ferrigan
**Designer:** Patrick Bonneville
**Consultant designer:** Philippe Hemono

**Cover design:** Patrick Bonneville
**Back cover text:** Shannon Partridge
**Cover picture:** UN Photo/Marco Dormino
**Half Title Page:** UN Photo/Marco Dormino
**Full Title Page:** Chris Vika/dreamstime.com



Printed and bound in China

ISBN 978-1-926654-02-7

Legal deposit - Bibliothèques et Archives nationales du Québec, 2010

Legal deposit - Library and Archives Canada, 2010

Series created by Patrick Bonneville

Produced with the support of Quebec Refundable Tax Credit for book Production Services and Sodexport program.

SODEC
Québec

"*The pursuit of peace and progress cannot end in a few years in either victory or defeat. The pursuit of peace and progress, with its trials and errors, its successes and setbacks, can never be relaxed and never abandoned.*"
—*Dag Hammarskjold*

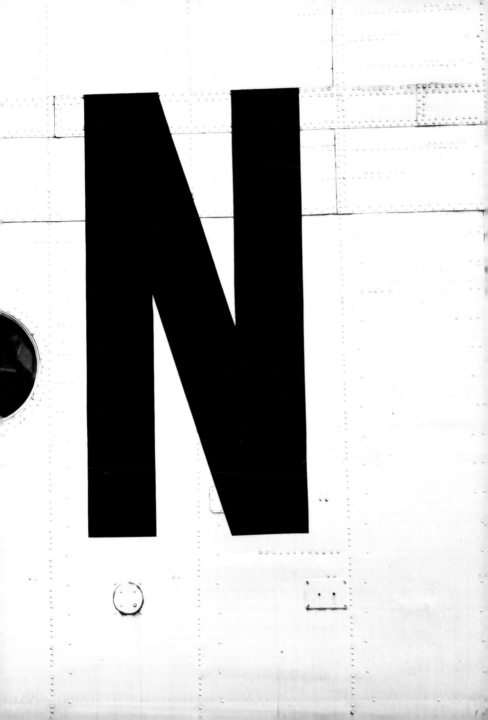

# CONTENTS

Photo credit: Angela Campanelli

highly visible and ultra-discreet, merit recognition and honor for their efforts to improve life for humankind.

For the most part, the employees, volunteers, and supporters of these organizations are neither superstars nor celebrities. Most of their leaders are unknown to us, as are the founders. Those who make these organizations viable are our global heroes, many of them working far away from the spotlight to make everyday life better and safer. They might be your neighbors. They might be family members. Maybe they are you. If this is the case, let me take this opportunity to humbly thank you. Thank you all. You are my heroes. This book is about your work and what you and your peers have accomplished.

The world would be a very dark place without you. You are an inspiration and you are hope.

You belong on humanity's Wall of Honor.

Patrick Bonneville

Every day, all over the planet, international organizations of all kinds are hard at work building a stronger, fairer, and safer world. They want to make sure that humanity doesn't fall into chaos. They want to create a world where the vulnerable are protected and where all people live in harmony with each other and with their environment. The charities, foundations, political groups, governmental, and non-governmental organizations (NGOs) that work for the betterment of our planet are, today, humanity's greatest assets.

Some of these organizations are legendary; some are known only to the people whose lives they touch. I hope that this book will introduce readers to many of the latter. Because all these groups,

## The Ranking Process

Many publishing folk and friends have asked me about the top-100 format of the HUMANITY books. Why do we choose a subjective ranking process? Well, here is my most honest answer: we want to make a statement. By listing these organizations in a preferential order, we can put emphasis on the ones we think are worth the most attention.

Ranking also creates debate. We want people to think more about these organizations and talk about them more. Ranking leads us to challenge and defend what is important to us and to humanity. Ranking the Wall of Honor challenges our humanitarian values, deep down inside.

On the other hand, our ranking is certainly not absolute truth. We acknowledge our Western bias. We acknowledge the limitations of our research. Nevertheless, there are thousands of great NGOs and international bodies making unarguable contributions to our world, and we hope our research reflects our appreciation of their work.

In Wall of Honor, we suggest that the top 3 or the top 10 organizations are wholly in their own league. The way we see it, these are organizations that the world just couldn't function without. We believe that some of these organizations are indeed more important to humanity than the others because of their history, their scope of activities, the size of their membership, and the extent of their reach in the world.

Moreover, by ranking 100 international humanitarian organizations, we create some room at the end of the list to include some lesser known organizations that are doing very important work. They might simply be lower-profile than the others because they were founded more recently.

We chose to apply five criteria in ranking the Wall of Honor:

### Past accomplishments
What has the organization accomplished so far? Is it relevant? Has it made a real difference?

### International reach
How many countries does the organization reach? Where are its employees from? Does it have a real impact on people's lives?

### Tangibility
How tangible is the relief the organization brings to the people in need?

### Peace and hope
Does the organization bring peace to people? Does it create a sense of hope in the world through the services it provides and by the image it reflects?

### Building a better world
Does the organization help to build a better and stronger world?

*"The Charter of the United Nations which you have just signed is a solid structure upon which we can build a better world. History will honor you for it. Between the victory in Europe and the final victory, in this most destructive of all wars, you have won a victory against war itself... With this Charter the world can begin to look forward to the time when all worthy human beings may be permitted to live decently as free people."*
*—President of the United States Harry S. Truman, addressing the final session at the San Francisco Conference, June 26, 1945.*

*Patrick Bonneville: We need the UN to make our world work; united people will put aside fighting to work together for their common objectives. The United Nations reflects the complicated human reality, where different countries have different cultures, different interests, and different ways of understanding the world. Nevertheless, UN member nations share the same goal: they want peace and security. All its members have the right to speak up and express their needs, but they want the UN to work. It is a complicated system, but I strongly believe in it and I support it with all my heart.*

*Even though we have decided to treat some of the United Nations' programs and divisions separately, we believe the UN as a single entity deserves top place on our list of honorable organizations.*

*"More than ever before in human history, we share a common destiny. We can master it only if we face it together. And that, my friends, is why we have the United Nations."*
—Kofi Annan

The name "United Nations" was chosen by Franklin D. Roosevelt and Winston Churchill to refer to the World War II allied forces. Inspired by the post-World War I League of Nations, an organization designed to promote peaceful cooperation and pooled resources, the United Nations referred to a 1942 declaration between allies in which they agreed to negotiate peace with the Axis alliance as a collective— as the United Nations. After the war, fifty states met in San Francisco to develop a charter, and on October 24, 1945, the United Nations saw the light of day. It was a fresh presence in the world that would change the way leaders think, govern, and cooperate. That very day, humanity regrouped.

In 2005, the Human Security Report from the University of British Columbia's Human Security Centre suggested that UN-related efforts were responsible for the decline—almost by half—in the number of wars, genocides, and human rights abuses since the end of the Cold War. UN organizations have contributed to maintaining fair laws and peace and security in the world. They have done this through various programs and agencies promoting democracy, economic development, human rights, and by ensuring environmental stability, strengthening international law, providing emergency relief after

**Left:** New York City, and the future site of the United Nations headquarters.
**Right:** Members of the Nigerian battalion of the United Nations-African Union Hybrid Mission in Darfur (UNAMID).

disasters, facilitating access to health care and HIV/AIDS programs, fighting drug abuse, and providing relief and development for refugees, the poor, the hungry, women, and other groups without a voice in much of the world.

The heart of the United Nations beats on First Avenue in the Turtle Bay neighborhood of Manhattan, New York City. One hundred and ninety-one countries—nearly every sovereign state in the world—meet there to try to achieve consensus on strategies for creating world peace and social and economic progress. There are UN offices in Geneva, Nairobi, and Vienna, with many others scattered around the world.

The UN is organized as five central divisions: the General Assembly, the Security Council, the Economic and Social Council (ECOSOC), the Secretariat, and the International Court of Justice. The General Assembly is the forum of exchange for all member nations, where they conven at regular intervals under a president elected from the membership. The Assembly deliberates and votes on matters such as executive staffing for divisions, budgeting, admission and suspension of members, and recommendations on peace and security. A two-thirds majority vote is required for a motion to pass, and the Assembly is not mandated to enforce recommendations, merely to extend them.

**Left:** Two blue berets showing young Haitian children how to brush their teeth properly.
**Right:** A member of the United Nations Stabilization Mission in Haiti (MINUSTAH) carries an infant to safety.

The Security Council's mandate is to receive complaints from UN member states about threats to peace. It is composed of five permanent core states: China, France, Russia, the United Kingdom, and the United States, plus ten other member states who serve two-year terms on the Council. United Nations Security Council resolutions are deliberated by the members and are presented as enforceable, binding decisions. The five permanent members can veto resolutions, but not the debates that precede them.

The Secretariat is the administrative and research body of the UN. Under the Secretary-General and Secretariat staff,

the division provides all the resources—material and information—required for the meetings of the other divisions. The division also oversees the administration of peacekeeping missions, conferences, and the implementation of Security Council resolutions. As the leader of the entire UN organization, the Secretary-General is generally considered a moderator for peace, and may propose Security Council intervention when he or she deems it necessary. His or her appointment as Secretary-General is proposed by the Security Council and voted by the General Assembly, usually for one or two terms of office of five years.

The fifty Economic and Social Council members meet once a year for a four-week session to deliberate and make recommendations on international economic and social cooperation and development initiatives. ECOSOC's president is usually voted to office for a one-year term from among the smaller powers represented in its membership. One of ECOSOC's main roles is to oversee the coherence of the UN bodies and organizations working in the domain of social and economic development.

The UN groups together a number of subsidiary organizations or agencies that perform humanitarian work, provide security and help ensure peace, and develop economic and social programs.

**Right:** Patrol during a community meeting between UNAMID officials and Arab nomads.
**Opposite page:** Pope Benedict XVI pays tribute to fallen United Nations staff , New York City.

Some of the better known organizations are entered seperately in *Wall of Honor,* including the International Atomic Energy Agency, the World Food Program, the United Nations Educational, Scientific and Cultural Organization, World Health Organization, World Bank, and others.

The United Nations is also well known for its peacekeeping missions. As distinguished from peacebuilding and peacemaking, peacekeeping is defined by the United Nations as "a way to help countries torn by conflict create conditions for sustainable peace." Peacekeepers, or "blue berets" for their blue berets or helmets, are soldiers, police officers, and other civilian personnel who monitor and observe peace processes in regions emerging from conflict. UN peacekeepers also support opposing sides in respecting the peace agreements they may have signed.

IN THE CAUSE OF PEACE

**Left:** Barack Obama, before his presidential election, with Secretary-General Ban Ki-moon.
**Right:** Helicopter prepares to pick up members of the Indian battalion of the United Nations Organization Mission in the Democratic Republic of the Congo (MONUC).

UN peacekeepers do not constitute an independent standing army. Troops from member nations serve under UN operational control. The reach of peacekeeping extends beyond the military aspect of the mission, however. "Multidimensional" involvement means UN peacekeepers may develop a transitional environment that is safe for citizens by performing human rights monitoring, supporting institutional reforms in governance and policing, and facilitating the disarmament and reintegration of former combatants. While a military presence is the major thrust of UN peacekeeping, operations also include administrators, economists, police officers, lawyers, electoral observers, land-mine specialists, and experts in communications.

United Nations peacekeeping has evolved as inter-state conflict has tended toward intra-state conflict. The forces are increasingly called to deploy to remote, uncertain operating environments and into volatile political contexts. Missions are also increasingly politically complex and more expensive. Regardless of circumstances, UN peacekeeping operations are typified by impartiality, non-use of force except in self-defence, and defence of the UN's mandate.

In 1997, after just over fifty years of existence, the United Nations was in need of some adjustments. An official reform program was initiated by former Secretary-General Kofi Annan, who presented a major report including recommendations that would make UN bureaucracy more transparent, accountable, and efficient.

One of the greatest recent achievements of the United Nations is the Millennium Summit, an international conference whose purpose was to discuss the role of the United Nations at the turn of the twenty-first century. At the time of the meeting, it was the largest gathering of world leaders in history. The result was the Millennium Development Goals (MDGs), eight international development goals that 192 United Nations member states and at least 23 international organizations have agreed to achieve by the year 2015. The objectives include reducing extreme poverty and child mortality rates, fighting disease epidemics such as AIDS, and developing a global partnership for development.

| Past accomplishments | 10/10 |
| International reach | 10/10 |
| Tangibility | 10/10 |
| Peace and hope | 9/10 |
| Building a better world | 10/10 |
| | |
| Average score | 9.8/10 |

*Patrick Bonneville: Red Cross and Red Crescent are in their own league. The organization is everywhere, in every country, ready to help those in need when the time comes. Their fast mobilization in Haiti is an example for other organizations. They are ready to help you when war hits your region. They are ready to provide you shelter when disasters tear apart your home.*

There are 186 individual national Red Cross and Red Crescent Societies (national branches) around the world, served by 97 million volunteers and 300,000 full-time employees. When war breaks out or an earthquake tears down a city, when a fire ravages a whole neighborhood or a tsunami erases villages from the surface of the Earth, when a plane crashes or a ship goes down, Red Cross and Red Crescent volunteers are very often the first to respond. The organization's seven principles say it all about this NGO:

humanity, impartiality, neutrality, independence, voluntary service, unity, and universality.

The roots of the movement go back to the nineteenth century, to 1859, when Swiss businessman Henry Dunant was on his way to Solferino to meet the French Emperor Napoleon III. In Solferino, he got caught in the middle of a battle of the Austro-Sardinian War. In one evening, in that small town of Solferino, Dunant witnessed 40,000 soldiers die and many others left wounded without help. Dunant spent days there helping the wounded on both sides. That trip changed his life. Back in his hometown, Dunant created an organization to provide basic care to all wounded soldiers. In 1863, in Geneva,

**Below:** American Red Cross National Headquarters in Washington, DC.
**Right:** Jan. 29, 2010. Haitian Red Cross volunteer Ralph Toussaint with Kengo Jean at Camp Simon, Port-au-Prince, Haiti.

Henry Dunant founded the International Committee for Relief to the Wounded. The book *A Memory of Solferino*, written and published by Dunant himself in 1862, recounts this story in detail.

Shortly after its creation, the group organized a small international conference in Geneva to agree on measures to provide basic care on battlefields. One year later, in 1864, the group organized a second, bigger conference with delegates from every European country and from Brazil, the United States, and Mexico. The first Geneva Convention was adopted, with the aim: "The amelioration of the condition of the wounded and sick in armed forces in the field." That same year, the first red cross emblem was used on a battlefield by the Dutch army. The Red Cross was born.

The cross emblem had connotations that were not appreciated elsewhere in the world, however. Taking into consideration its Muslim soldiers' beliefs, the Ottoman Empire came up with the red crescent symbol during the Russo-Turkish War between 1876 and 1878. The Red Cross agreed with the initiative, approving the use of the red crescent for non-Christian countries.

**Opposite page:** Iranian Red Crescent worker deployed to Haiti in the relief and health sectors.
**Left:** Red Cross worker on the front line after the 2010 Haiti earthquake.
**Below:** Red Cross worker providing necessary care to a young infant in Haiti, January 2010

Since then, the Red Cross and the Red Crescent have helped save the lives of millions. On October 15, 1914, immediately after the start of World War I, the Red Cross set up its International Prisoners-of-War (POW) Agency. By the end of the war, due to the intervention of the agency, about 200,000 prisoners were exchanged between the warring parties, released from captivity, and returned to their home country.

Other examples of how the Red Cross has contributed to humanity abound. On August 6, 1945, a nuclear weapon hit the ground in Japan. Just few hours

later, the Red Cross, led by doctor Marcel Junod, was in operation at the hospital in Hiroshima. There were eighty-four patients, ten nurses, and twenty students to help. More recently, in December 2004, when Southeast Asia was hit by the worst tsumani in that region in ages, the Red Cross-Red Crescent raised a staggering $3 billion. In 2005, after the passage of Hurricane Katrina through New Orleans, the American Red Cross opened 1,470 different shelters and registered 3.8 million overnight stays. A total of 244,000 Red Cross workers were utilized during this difficult period. In 2006, there were 1,960 full-time Red Cross staff in Sudan, helping Darfur's refugees. In January 2010, the Red Cross helped thousands of Haitians who lost their homes and loved ones after the earthquake that devastated the country.

As one of the most recognized organizations in the world, the Red Cross-Red Crescent has been awarded three Nobel Peace Prizes, in 1917, 1944, and 1963. The organization currently has about 97 million members and volunteers throughout the world, including some 20 million active volunteers.

**Above:** Getting first aid service in Haiti.
**Right:** Landing near refugee camps in Africa.

*"I remember with emotion the assistance given to the victims on both sides of the front line during the Rwandan conflict. The injured were treated in that place, without anyone asking them what ethnic group they belonged to, whereas outside craziness embraced the whole country."*
—Aline Mukamabano, the first local employee to be hired by the ICRC in Rwanda, in 1990

*"Would it not be possible, in time of peace and quiet, to form relief societies for the purpose of having care given to the wounded in wartime by zealous, devoted and thoroughly qualified volunteers?"*
—Jean Henri Dunant

| | |
|---|---|
| Past accomplishments | 10/10 |
| International reach | 10/10 |
| Tangibility | 10/10 |
| Peace and hope | 8.5/10 |
| Building a better world | 10/10 |
| Average score | 9.7/10 |

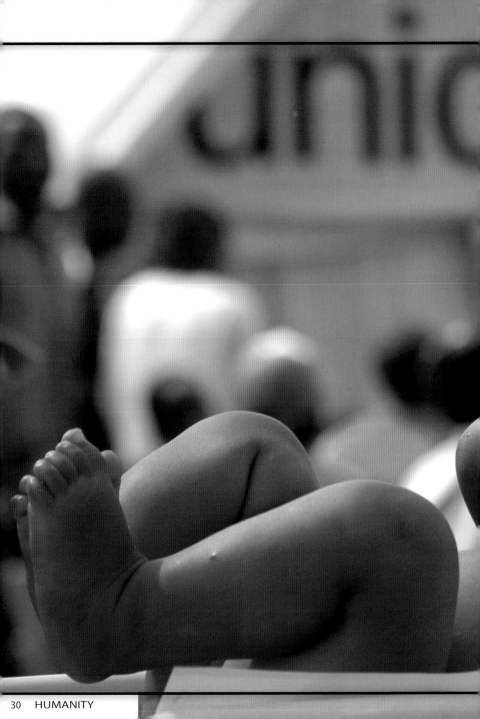

*Patrick Bonneville: If the Red Cross is the mother of NGOs, then UNICEF is the mother of all children in the world. It gives us a certain peace of mind to know that UNICEF is working on behalf of the world's children, making sure none of them is left behind.*

For over half a century, the United Nations Children's Fund (UNICEF) has been working hard around the world to better the lives of children and their mothers, especially those in the developing world. On December 11, 1946, the United Nations General Assembly created UNICEF to provide humanitarian and developmental assistance in the form of emergency food and healthcare to children in countries devastated by World War II. The need for this kind of work continued, however, and in 1953, UNICEF became a permanent agency of the UN; until that time it had been called the United Nations International Children's Emergency Fund, the basis for the acronym it still goes by today.

UNICEF programs are oriented toward the survival and development of children, protection from violence,

**Left:** A displaced girl queues with adults for food during a distribution in Chota Lahore Camp in North-West Frontier Province (NWFP) of Pakistan.
**Right:** Every year, nearly 11 million children die from preventable causes before reaching their fifth birthday.

exploitation, and abuse, HIV/AIDS affecting children, policy advocacy and partnerships for children's rights, and basic education and gender equality, including education for girls.

A significant milestone in UNICEF's history was in 1959, when the UN General Assembly adopted the Declaration of the Rights of the Child, which defines children's rights to protection, education, health care, shelter, and good nutrition. Another was in 1989, when the Convention on the Rights of the Child was ratified by the General Assembly. One of the most rapidly and widely accepted human rights treaties in history, its signatories are obligated to uphold its tenets and are monitored for adherence. It specifies the civil, political, economic, social, and cultural rights of children. It was ratified by every member state in the United Nations except for Somalia and the United States, who have nevertheless committed to an intention to sign.

UNICEF's goodwill ambassador program advances the cause for children through celebrity spokespeople, such as David Beckham, Shakira, Roger Federer, Mia Farrow, Liv Tyler, Jessica Sarah Parker, Joel Madden, Lucy Liu, and Ewan McGregor. They bring support, advocate, and attract media attention to the plight of children.

*"I'm Mia Farrow and I believe that all children have a right to grow up in health, peace and dignity."*
*—Mia Farrow, UNICEF Goodwill Ambassador*

| Past accomplishments | 9/10 |
| International reach | 10/10 |
| Tangibility | 10/10 |
| Peace and hope | 9/10 |
| Building a better world | 10/10 |
| Average score | 9.6/10 |

**Left:** A girl carries her baby brother in front of tents, at a camp in the town of Bulucheke, Uganda.
**Above:** UNICEF Ambassador Lucy Liu in DRC.

According to UNICEF, its Foundation Principles are:

*Non-discrimination* - all children, in all situations, all of the time, everywhere, have the same right to develop their potential.

*The best interests of the child* - a primary consideration, the best interests of the child must be considered in all actions and decisions affecting him or her.

*The right to survival and development* - it is essential to ensure access to basic services and strive for justice in order for children to achieve their full development.

*The views of the child* - children's voices must be heard and be respected in all matters concerning their own rights. Children must retain active, free, and meaningful contribution in the decisions affecting them.

Children of the Western world participate themselves in one of its most recognized fundraising drives; every Halloween, children hang the orange UNICEF box around their necks to collect coins while trick-or-treating. The campaign was first used in the early 1950s in Philadelphia. To date, American children have collected over $132 million with the boxes.

UNICEF was awarded the Nobel Peace Prize in 1965 and the Prince of Asturias Award of Concord in 2006.

*"In a global economy worth over $30 trillion, it is clear that the necessary resources and know-how to reach every child are well within our grasp."*
—*Carol Bellamy, former Executive Director of UNICEF*

**Above:** After the 2004 Indian Ocean tsunami, UNICEF and its partners created and furnished hundreds of temporary learning centers, supplied textbooks to 830,000 children, and paid teacher salaries for six months.

In 1971, in the aftermath of the Nigerian-Biafran War, a small group of French doctors banded together to provide medical care for people regardless of race, religion, creed, or political affiliation. At around the same time, another group of French doctors was recruiting medical help for a cyclone that had killed 500,000 in East Pakistan, now Bangladesh. The two organizations joined forces and Médecins Sans Frontières, or "doctors without borders," was born.

With a new international mandate, Médecins Sans Frontières (MSF) immediately intervened in Managua, the capital of Nicaragua, after the devastating 1972 earthquake destroyed most of the city and killed an estimated 30,000 people. Since then it has intervened around the world by working with governments, militaries, and pharmaceutical companies to bring an end to injustices in meeting medical needs. It maintains dialogues with local authorities and aid agencies to ensure the best possible course of action for the situation at hand. The organization has grown to include associations in Australia, Austria, Belgium, Canada, Denmark, France, Germany, Greece, Holland, Hong Kong, Italy, Japan, Luxembourg, Norway, Spain, Sweden, Switzerland, the United Kingdom, and the United States.

MSF documentation shows that in 2006, MSF teams performed more than 9 million outpatient consultations, hospitalized almost half a million patients, delivered 99,000 babies, treated

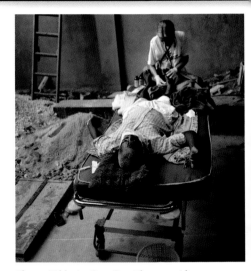

**Above:** Médecins Sans Frontières provides emergency medical assistance to populations in danger in more than 70 countries.
**Right:** Médecins Sans Frontières office in Darfur.

1.8 million people for malaria, treated 150,000 malnourished children, provided 100,000 people living with HIV/AIDS with antiretroviral therapy, vaccinated 1.8 million people against meningitis, and conducted 64,000 surgeries.

The organization also prioritizes access to medical tools, medicine, and vaccines for on-the-ground medical personnel and publicly takes positions that will ensure proper health care for refugees, as it did during the Ethiopian government's displacement of hundreds of thousands of people in the 1980s. After the 1994 genocide in Rwanda, MSF called for an international military response, and it also condemned the Serbian massacre of civilians at

"*The globalization of compassion and of human rights is a sign of substantial moral progress.*"
—*Bernard Kouchner*

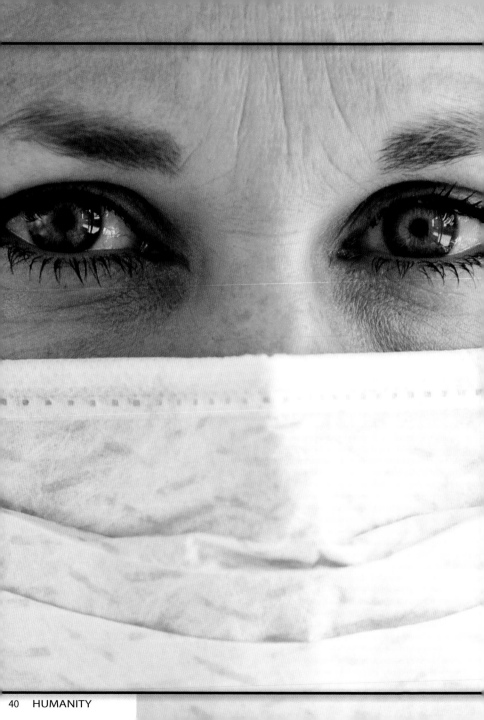

Srebrenica in 1995. MSF publicly denounced the Russian attack on Grozny, the Chechen capital, in 1999, and drew the world's attention to the Darfur crisis at the United Nations Security Council in 2004 and 2005.

As further testimony to its role in improving the lives of people around the world, in 1999, MSF received the Nobel Peace Prize. The prize money served to finance research into treatments for diseases typical in the world's poorest countries, drugs that provide less profit to the pharmaceutical industry.

**Left:** The average mission period is six months.
**Above:** Bernard Kouchner

### Médecins du Monde (Doctors of the World)

Médecins Sans Frontières founding member, Dr. Bernard Kouchner, was vocal about the atrocities he encountered. His desire to make a positive change in the world through medicine was accompanied by an increasing desire to take a political stance rather than one of neutrality. His ideals drifted from the initial purpose of MSF, and in 1980 he left to develop a new enterprise: Médecins du Monde, or "doctors of the world."

Along with fifteen other French doctors, Kouchner created MDM as a non-governmental humanitarian aid organization that would bear witness and make public the atrocities that aid workers actually see and experience. MDM holds that humanitarian work cannot be separated from politics without leaving room for the potential for abuses of the aid by leaders in the countries in question.

MDM is present in more than eighty countries and has participated in about 300 relief projects. It is active in three areas: short-term emergency aid, reconstruction and rehabilitation aid, and long-term development projects lasting up to three years. MDM has a strong volunteer base of about 6,700 people and about 360 staff members. The great majority of its budget is spent directly on relief efforts.

| | |
|---|---|
| Past accomplishments | 9/10 |
| International reach | 9/10 |
| Tangibility | 10/10 |
| Peace and hope | 10/10 |
| Building a better world | 9.5/10 |
| | |
| Average score | 9.5/10 |

*Kimberly Murray: The giant panda mascot of the WWF is instantly recognizable. It is Chi-Chi from the London zoo, who died in 1972.*

Formerly named the World Wildlife Fund, WWF is a non-profit conservation fund that works to preserve and restore the environment through research and conservation projects around the world.

In 1961, a group of conservationists were inspired to create "Nature's Red Cross," a group that would "halt and reverse the destruction of our environment." Originally an initiative to help the fund-strapped World Conservation Union, or IUCN, the WWF opened an office on September 11, 1961, in Morges, Switzerland. In under half a century, the WWF has grown in its own right into an international network of over ninety offices in forty countries. Sixty percent of its budget comes from donations by private individuals. It is the world's largest independent conservation organization with over 5 million supporters and involvement in 1,300 conservation and environment projects.

WWF aims to halt the degradation of the planet's natural environment and build a future in which humans live in harmony with nature; this means ensuring that the use of renewable natural resources is sustainable and that pollution and wasteful consumption are reduced. Its work lobbying for new laws and business practices is a significant contribution to the planet's ongoing biological diversity.

WWF also concentrates its efforts on the conservation of the world's biodiversity: forests, freshwater ecosystems, and oceans and coasts. The fund specifically focuses on the conservation of thirty-six plant and animal species which are essential to their ecosystems, as well as thirty-five "eco-regions," such as the Arctic and the Amazon rainforest. WWF also has the goal to reduce the carbon footprint of humans in six specific areas: carbon emissions, cropland, grazing land, fishing, forestry, and water. To this end, WWF has negotiated "debt-for-nature" swaps with governments. This is a plan whereby a portion of a nation's debt is converted into funds for conservation. Participating countries include Ecuador, Madagascar, the Philippines, and Zambia.

As an indication of humanity's appreciation for the intentions and efforts of WWF, its Web site welcomed over 5.5 million visitors in 2008, from 236 countries and territories.

*"We shan't save all we should like to, but we shall save a great deal more than if we had never tried."*
*—Sir Peter Scott, one of the founders of WWF*

**Right:** WWF demonstration at the 2009 United Nations Climate Change Conference, also known as the Copenhagen Summit.

| Past accomplishments | 10/10 |
| --- | --- |
| International reach | 10/10 |
| Tangibility | 8/10 |
| Peace and hope | 7.5/10 |
| Building a better world | 10/10 |
| | |
| Average score | 9.1/10 |

*Patrick Bonneville: Photos of big UN planes and giant trucks delivering food bags are very strong inspirational images. They tell a story of poverty and misfortune, but they also contain a story about people risking their lives in order to deliver food to others.*

The United Nations' World Food Program (WFP) is the world's largest humanitarian organization. Its goal is to get food to the hungry in emergency situations and prevent hunger in the future. It delivers food to 90 million people per year, 58 million of them children.

Created in 1960 at the suggestion of the UN's Food and Agricultural Organization, the WFP was established as a multilateral food aid agency. Its goal is to address malnutrition and hunger, especially that of children. The ultimate objective of the organization, naturally, is to work toward the elimination of the very need for aid itself. It works toward this by providing food that will allow refugees to survive, that will improve the quality of life of people in desperate situations, and that will help people be physcially and mentally ready to learn long-term sustainability practices. The WFP also delivers work programs that help communities in building self-reliance.

The process for getting food to the hungry involves many steps. First, WFP Food Security Analysts visit the region in question to find out who is hungry, where, and why. They also try to understand how people will be further affected if crisis or conflict worsens. Next, experts decide how to tailor the food aid to resemble the typical diet and fill people's nutritional needs. The food is then bought by the WFP's procurement managers, who strive to buy as much as possible from sources close to the problem. In sometimes complex

**Opposite page:** Dropping food by planes when access by other means is impossible.
**Upper left:** Warehouse in Haiti, in which civilians are receiving food and water rations distributed by the World Food Programme (WFP) in the aftermath of Hurricane Ike.
**Right:** Food donated by the World Food Programme (WFP), for distribution to Haitian victims of the Tropical Storm Hanna.

logistical circumstances, the food is then transported to the region; since at least half of WFP-sourced food comes from within the country where it is needed, local means of transport are utilized. The other half, sourced internationally, is delivered by sea to a nearby port.

Another important step in the WFP mission includes providing meals to students in their schools; for many it is the only nutritious meal they will receive in a day. In some regions, the WFP offers "take-home" rations such as cooking oil or rice to families who send their daughters to school. In its Food for Assets program, workers are given food in exchange for time spent working on local infrastructure projects or learning sustainable living skills. The WFP also works with other organizations to adapt food aid, where possible, to the nutritional needs created by HIV/AIDs. It also has HIV/AIDS programs in over fifty countries to support treatment, care, and livlihood security.

The WFP's headquarters are located in Rome, although it has more than eighty offices worldwide. It employs 12,000 people, 92 percent of whom work in the field. The WFP works in partnership with about 3,000 NGOs around the world. Its budget is made up of donations and funding from the Central Emergency Response Fund. The organization also accepts food and items necessary to grow and prepare food. The agency parters with other UN groups such as the FAO and the International Fund for Agricultural Development, as well as with national governments and other NGOs.

*"Food security is not only a matter of humanitarian assistance and agricultural development; it is a matter of national security, peace and stability."*
—*WFP Executive Director Josette Sheeran*

**Above:** Distribution to the victims of a tropical storm.
**Upper right:** A woman and a child receive emergency rations being distributed by the World Food Programme at a warehouse operated by CARE.
**Opposite page:** Some 93 percent of WFP funding goes either to cover food costs or to pay for its transport.

| | |
|---|---|
| Past accomplishments | 10/10 |
| International reach | 10/10 |
| Tangibility | 10/10 |
| Peace and hope | 8/10 |
| Building a better world | 7/10 |
| Average score | 9.0/10 |

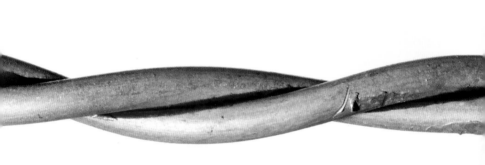

"Open your newspaper any day of the week and you will find a report from somewhere in the world of someone being imprisoned, tortured or executed because his opinions or religion are unacceptable to his government. The newspaper reader feels a sickening sense of impotence. Yet if these feelings of disgust all over the world could be united into common action, something effective could be done."
—Peter Benenson, founder of Amnesty International

*Patrick Bonneville: With the United Nations, we succeeded in establishing universal human rights that must be respected by all states and governments. But because of human nature, the greatest challenge is to have these rights respected all over the world. I find it very comforting to know there are organizations such as Amnesty International and Human Rights Watch. We can count on them to bring to light human rights abuses.*

Amnesty International was created in July 1961 by London lawyer Peter Benenson, after he read about two Portuguese men who were jailed for publicly making a toast to liberty. In "An Appeal for Amnesty, 1961," Benenson and his early partners aimed to rally support for "prisoners of conscience," or those men and women who are persecuted by their governments for their opinions or religion.

In 1962, the group officially became known as Amnesty International. At the time, it concentrated on a campaign of "Threes:" groups of local activist supporters would conduct research and letter campaigns for three prisoners of conscience—one each from a communist, capitalist, and developing nation—who had not made use of violence. They would also advocate in general for compliance by countries to sections 18 and 19 of the United Nations Declarations of Human Rights, which affirm the right of all individuals to freedom of thought, conscience, and religion, as well as the right to freedom of opinion and expression.

AI maintains complete independence from any political ideology or association and is financially self-sufficient; this is necessary in order to effectively lobby against political opposition and restrictions to press freedom and for the rights of individuals to asylum and to a timely public trial before impartial courts.

The non-profit AI relies solely on donations from its 2.2 million members and supporters from 150 countries, who raise its nearly $47 million operating budget. Its members come from all walks of life, with widely different political and religious views. They are, however, united by a determination to work for a world where everyone can exercise their rights

**Left:** Campaign against Guantanamo Bay.
**Above:** Campaign "UN: Act Now For Iran"

to free thought and expression. Amnesty International believes that every individual supporter makes a difference and that solidarity simply keeps hope alive for prisoners of conscience.

Some of AI's broadened objectives today are to "stop violence against women and children, defend the rights and dignity of those trapped in poverty, abolish the death penalty, oppose torture and combat terror with justice, free prisoners of conscience, protect the rights of refugees and migrants, and regulate the global arms trade." To this end, the organization "researches and generates action to prevent and end grave abuses of human rights and to demand justice for those whose rights have been violated." Members and supporters "exert influence on governments, political bodies, companies and intergovernmental groups," and activists mobilize public pressure through mass demonstrations, vigils, and direct lobbying as well as online and offline campaigning.

Sixteen years after its foundation, in 1977, Amnesty International was awarded the Nobel Peace Prize for its work in bringing peace to the world.

*"Injustice anywhere is a threat to justice everywhere. We are caught in an inescapable network of mutuality, tied in a single garment of destiny. Whatever affects one directly, affects all indirectly."*
—Martin Luther King, jr.

| | |
|---|---|
| Past accomplishments | 9/10 |
| International reach | 9/10 |
| Tangibility | 8/10 |
| Peace and hope | 9/10 |
| Building a better world | 9.5/10 |
| Average score | 8.9/10 |

**Left:** Campaigning in Washington, DC.
**Above:** Amnesty in West Bengal, India, 2008.
**Right:** Firing up the Amnesty International logo in Berlin, Germany, December 10, 2008.

*Patrick Bonneville: When there is an outbreak of disease, when there is an environmental health threat, medical authorities and the public from all around the world turn to one institution, the World Health Organization. When the avian flu, SARS, and H1N1 hit the world, the WHO got things under control.*

The United Nations' World Health Organization (WHO) is recognized as the international authority on public health. It was established in 1948 to research and advise on global health matters, implement international health norms and standards, and offer technical and concrete support. WHO currently counts 193 member states. Any country that is a member of the United Nations may join WHO by accepting its constitution.

Since poverty contributes greatly to poor health, the WHO concentrates on efforts that will alleviate such conditions, regardless of culture, race, or creed. In poverty-stricken and rural areas, people have less access to health care workers. That means that survival rates for mothers and children are low, during childbirth and after, and it means that otherwise preventable diseases take hold.

Worldwide, there are 59.8 million healthcare professionals; nevertheless, experts say they are in short supply in most of the world. An incredible 4.2 million more healthcare workers are required to ensure adequate care for all. Africa alone is in dire need of some 1.5 million professionals, and without prompt action, the situation will worsen.

Specifically, the WHO names its objectives as the following: to provide leadership on matters critical to health and engage in partnerships where joint action is needed; shape the research agenda and stimulate the generation, translation, and dissemination of relevant knowledge; set norms and standards and promote and monitor their implementation; propose ethical and evidence-based policy options; provide technical support and build sustainable institutional capacity; and monitor health trends. The organization is bound by the UN's Millennium Development Goals for the prevention and treatment of chronic and tropical diseases.

**Left:** WHO employee collects health information from households in Niger during a severe food shortage crisis.
**Right:** In the field to monitor the H1N1 pandemic.

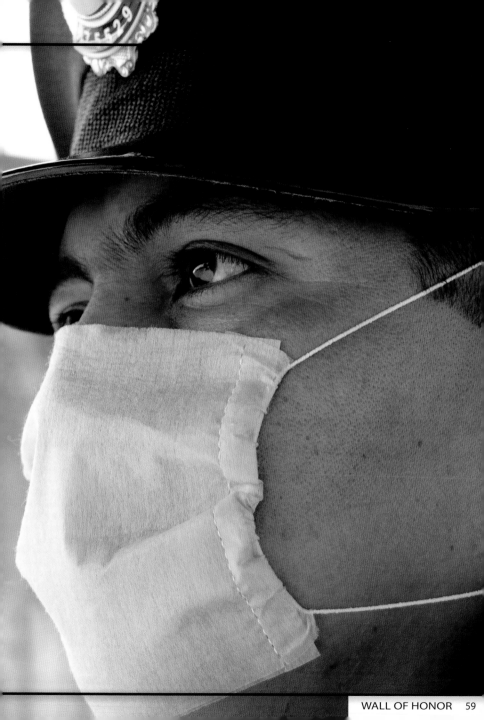

Past accomplishments        10/10
International reach          10/10
Tangibility                 10/10
Peace and hope               7/10
Building a better world      7/10

Average score               8.8/10

Among other successes, the WHO has supported programs that developed and distributed an effective smallpox vaccine. After two decades of fighting the disease, it was declared in 1980 that it had been eradicated, a first in human history. The WHO also estimates that polio will be eradicated within our lifetime. The organization's *HIV/AIDS Toolkit for Zimbabwe* is now an international standard for fighting the illness. And on its website, WHO reports that twenty-seven countries have seen a reduction of malaria cases by 50 percent between 1990 and 2006. It also notes that for the same time period, 5.7 billion people gained acces to safe drinking water, an increase from 4.1 billion.

**Opposite page:** UN Secretary-General Ban Ki-moon and Margaret Chan, Director-General of the World Health Organization, at a video conference with WTO experts on the H1N1 influenza virus situation in different regions.
**Above:** WHO staff listening to a press conference by Margaret Chan on the H1N1 pandemic situation.
**Below:** WHO vaccination centre in Congo, 1962.

*Patrick Bonneville: This organization has one goal: to monitor, document and end human rights abuses around the globe. Its publications, especially* World Report, *are the result of their vigilance and provide objective descriptions of human rights violations. Human Rights Watch does not answer to or receive funding from any government or international authority. It is free to tell the world what is really going on, whether a country is rich or poor, democracy or autocracy. I highly respect this organization and its human rights advocates, who are extraordinary and peaceful freedom fighters.*

We live in a world where every single individual is supposed to have basic rights. Unfortunately, this is not the reality for a great many people. A number of independent organizations and governmental authorities work hard to make sure human rights are kept in the forefront of cultural and political practices everywhere. Human Rights Watch has become a strong leader and reference in that field.

The organization's roots go back to the 1970s when an important historical treaty, the Helsinki Accord, was signed in order to narrow the gap between the East and West. The objective was to reduce tensions that had arisen during the Cold War. As a result of this treaty, a special organization was created to monitor the Soviet Union with respect to its commitments. It was called Helsinki Watch, and it had a mandate to alert the media to human rights abuses in the Soviet Union. The watchdog approach to monitoring was found to be very effective.

Just a few years later, in the early 1980s, Americas Watch was created. The organization made a name for itself by exposing atrocities and human rights violations committed during the Central American civil wars, both on the part of rebels and government forces. Americas Watch stepped even further forward by pointing out the roles of foreign governments in these war crimes.

The number of organizations grew rapidly, and the late 1980s gave birth to Asia Watch, Africa Watch, and Middle East Watch. In 1988, they merged to become Human Rights Watch. Since then, the organization has had human rights experts working in the field and monitoring governments all over the world. More than 90 countries are monitored, especially those in crisis. Although Human Rights Watch is well respected by international law makers and has influence on national leaders, it remains independent in its mission.

Today, Human Rights Watch is a corps of nearly 300 human rights professionals from all over the world. They are lawyers, journalists, professors, and field experts. Together, they produce more than 100 reports and briefings every year on human rights conditions in about ninety countries; their findings feed international and national media reports and other organizations' efforts. At the end of each year, they publish the world's leading reference book about human rights, *World Report*. It summarizes human rights conditions in every country.

In 1997, the organization shared the Nobel Peace Prize as a founding member of the International Campaign to Ban Landmines. That campaign led to the 1999 Ottawa Treaty, a convention that aims to end the production and use of anti-personnel mines. So far, 156 nations have signed the treaty. More recently, in 2008, Human Rights Watch helped the United Nations create the Convention on Cluster Munitions, an international treaty that prohibits the use of cluster bombs. One hundred and four nations have signed that convention.

*"There is an enormous problem that when a government as influential as the United States flouts basic human rights standards, it undermines the standards and gives the green light to other governments to do the same."*
*—Kenneth Roth, Executive Director of Human Rights Watch*

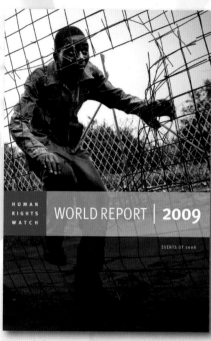

**Upper left:** HRW Emergencies Director Peter Bouckaert conducts interviews in Iraq, 2003. **Above:** Human Rights Watch's annual report. The *World Report* summarizes human rights conditions in the world.

| | |
|---|---|
| Past accomplishments | 8/10 |
| International reach | 10/10 |
| Tangibility | 7/10 |
| Peace and hope | 9/10 |
| Building a better world | 9/10 |
| Average score | 8.6/10 |

*Patrick Bonneville: When individuals and families are forced to flee, when they have no more home, the UNHCR takes over. It provides safety and shelter for those who have left everything behind.*

The Office of the High Commissioner for Refugees (UNHCR) is the United Nations refugee support agency. Refugees are people who have fled their homeland for fear of persecution that will not be mitigated by their own government. They are people searching for protection and survival, not just a better way of life.

Established in 1950, the agency's goal is to ensure safe asylum and safe refuge for all people who require it. The agency advocates for their basic needs, including their rights to freedom of religion and movement, to work and education, and to have access to travel documents. The UNHCR is not structured to correct the root causes that drive refugees from their countries, which may include military actions, a political uprising, or religious rebellions. Rather, they strive to aid those who are punished as a consequence of such events.

Through its strict guidelines, the UNHCR makes every effort to work with host governments in helping people restart their lives, either through local integration, resettlement in subsequent host countries, or through voluntary return to their homeland. An estimated 26 million internally displaced persons are helped by the UNHCR. Overall, the UNHCR offers aid to some 32 million people worldwide, about half of them refugees or asylum seekers. Refugees themselves are required to respect the laws and regulations of the country accepting them.

**Above:** A refugee holds his UNHCR registration card as he waits to receive food rations.
**Right:** UNHCR Goodwill Ambassador and actress Angelina Jolie

*"We cannot close ourselves off to information and ignore the fact that millions of people are out there suffering. I honestly want to help. I don't believe I feel differently from other people. I think we all want justice and equality, a chance for a life with meaning. All of us would like to believe that if we were in a bad situation someone would help us."*
*—Angelina Jolie, UNHCR Goodwill Ambassador, August 23, 2001*

The agency has expanded its area of concern to include the protection and humanitarian assistance of people not narrowly considered refugees but who, rather, are considered internally displaced persons (IDPs). These are people who have had to flee their homes but remain within their home country.

The UNHCR has twice been honored with the Nobel Peace Prize, in 1954 and in 1981. Through their Goodwill Ambassador program featuring recognizable public figures, important advances can be made for refugees. Current ambassadors are: actors Angelina Jolie, Osvaldo Laport, and Adel Imam; opera singers Barbara Hendricks and Boris Trajanov, fashion designer Giorgio Armani; novelist Khaled Hosseini, and folk and popular singers Julien Clerc, Muazzez Ersoy, and George Dalaras.

*"Although international law distinguishes between refugees and the internally displaced, such distinctions are absurd to those who have been forced from their homes and who have lost everything. Uprooted people are equally deserving of help whether they have crossed an international border or not."*
*—António Manuel de Oliveira Guterres, United Nations High Commissioner for Refugees, June 2009*

**Left:** A family in Bessian, Jammu and Kashmir, Pakistan at a tent city set up by the UNHCR.
**Above:** UNHCR works in 118 countries.
**Right:** Internally displaced persons (IDPs) inside a UN Refugee Agency (UNHCR) tent, in Beto Timur.

| | |
|---|---|
| Past accomplishments | 10/10 |
| International reach | 10/10 |
| Tangibility | 8/10 |
| Peace and hope | 6/10 |
| Building a better world | 8/10 |
| Average score | 8.4/10 |

*Patrick Bonneville: The United Nations' Declaration of Universal Human Rights might just be the most significant advance in human history. The United Nations High Commissioner for Human Rights is the guardian of this declaration, available in 375 languages. We consider it to be one of the most important documents in the world.*

The United Nations High Commissioner for Human Rights, also known simply as OHCHR, was established in 1993 for a world conference on human rights. Nations from all around the globe felt a need to create a strong human rights organization within the United Nations system. The basic roles of the OHCHR are to promote human rights and to address violations of these rights.

At the national and international levels, OHCHR works with legal representatives, other international organizations, and other UN bodies in order to monitor the laws and norms regarding human rights. Based in Geneva, OHCHR has eight regional offices in East Africa, Southern Africa, Central America, Latin America, South East Asia, the Middle East, and the Pacific.

The organization handles the human rights aspects of UN Peace missions in seventeen countries. It also has independent and impartial special registrars for specific regions or conflicts.

The OHCHR Rapid Response Unit is designed to quickly deploy to sudden human rights crises. This special unit is prepared to go into the field, monitor the situation, collect information, and report back to the United Nations on abuses. Since the creation of the unit in 2006, the group has been sent to Timor-Leste, Western Sahara, Liberia, Lebanon, and Beit-Hanoun, in the Occupied Palestinian Territories. In August 2003, the UN High Commissioner for Human Rights, Sérgio Vieira de Mello, died during the Iraq War when the Baghdad Canal Hotel was bombed by extremists.

Human Rights Day is celebrated on December 10, the date the Universal Declaration of Human Rights was signed in 1948.

| | |
|---|---|
| Past accomplishments | 8/10 |
| International reach | 10/10 |
| Tangibility | 7/10 |
| Peace and hope | 8.5/10 |
| Building a better world | 8/10 |
| Average score | 8.3/10 |

**Left:** Yung-wha Khang, Deputy High Commissioner for Human Rights, at the Human Rights Summit for Women Leaders in December 2009.
**Right:** René Cassin of France addressed the UN General Assembly, December 6, 1968. He received the Nobel Peace Prize the same year for his work in drafting the Universal Declaration of Human Rights

*Fiat panis!*—"Let there be bread!" This is the motto of the Food and Agriculture Organization of the United Nations, or the FAO. Created in 1945, the organization offers a framework for nations to negotiate accords and lobby for strategies to defeat hunger. The growing list of FAO members currently stands at 193 nations.

At the heart of their efforts is the goal of continuous and basic access to quality food for all societies. Their assistance is driven by the desire to share the skills that allow people to feed themselves by finding sustainable solutions to specific situations. To this end, the FAO facilitates the transmission of information and technology that helps developing nations gain access to improvements in agriculture, forestry, and fisheries. The FAO is ready with immediate action to counter urgent problems, while other programs are long-term development projects.

The FAO manages an annual budget of approximately $929.8 million, which is provided through member contribution. The budget covers all aspects of management of the organization, and through recent restructuring, an impressive $50 million a year has been saved.

*"It is hard to accept that in the 21st century millions of families are still living in poverty due to a lack of access to land, the most basic production resource."*
*—FAO Director-General Jacques Diouf*

**Above:** FAO Director-General Jacques Diouf speaking at the press conference for the closing session of the World Summit on Food Security, Rome, 2009.

**Left:** Farmer harvesting sorghum produced from seeds donated by the FAO.
**Above:** Delegates attend the opening session of the Civil Society Organizations Forum parallel to the World Summit on Food Security, Rome, 2009.

| | |
|---|---|
| Past accomplishments | 10/10 |
| International reach | 10/10 |
| Tangibility | 6.5/10 |
| Peace and hope | 6/10 |
| Building a better world | 9/10 |
| | |
| Average score | 8.3/10 |

# 13 - SAVE THE CHILDREN

*Patrick Bonneville: This organization was created by a beautiful woman who had passion, courage, and determination. Subsequent generations have continued her mission and have built one of the greatest international aid organizations in our world.*

**Above:** Save The Children helping children after the 2010 Haiti earthquake.
**Right:** Leogane, Haiti, January 24, 2010. Save The Children's Kathryn Bowles meets families in camps.

When World War I raged across Europe, children were left wounded and homeless by Allied blockades and bombing. British citizen Eglantyne Jebb, with the help of her sister Dorothy Buxton, saw little help and hope on the ground for children caught in the crossfire. In 1919 she founded a group that would pressure her government to end its role in the Allied blockade. She went on to advocate for universal measures that would ensure the safety of children everywhere by forming the International Save the Children Union, based in Geneva, Switzerland.

As she was drafting the Declaration of the Rights of the Child in 1924, several branches of Save the Children began to appear in other countries. Jebb's early initiatives were at the heart of the UN Convention on the Rights of the Child, adopted by the United Nations in 1989 and endorsed by nearly every country around the world. Today, in over 120 countries worldwide, 28 nonprofit organizations belong to the International Save the Children Alliance, which focuses on fighting for children's rights and on delivering immediate and lasting improvements for them no matter where they live.

As the organization itself says, "Save the Children wants a world which respects and values each child, a world which listens to children and learns, a world where all children have hope and opportunity."

| Past accomplishments | 8/10 |
|---|---|
| International reach | 8.5/10 |
| Tangibility | 9/10 |
| Peace and hope | 7.5/10 |
| Building a better world | 8.5/10 |
| | |
| Average score | 8.3/10 |

*"All wars, just or unjust, are waged against the child."*
*—Eglantyne Jebb, founder of Save The Children*

**Left:** Ellen Johnson Sirleaf, President of the Republic of Liberia, Geneva, 2006.
**Below:** Juan Somavia, Director-General of the ILO World Day against Child Labour, June 12th 2009.
**Opposite page:** A young girl works and lives in a brickyard near Islamabad, Pakistan.

The agency was awarded the Nobel Peace Prize in 1969 for its contribution to improving work conditions.

The International Labor Organization (ILO) is a specialized agency of the United Nations whose mandate is to advocate for humane work conditions for people around the globe. Its 180 member states have ratify conventions that become treaties international when a minimum number of governments have signed. Their conventions and recommendations are referred to as the International Labour Code.

Originally founded as an agency of the League of Nations after World War I, the ILO has developed conventions and standards that address child labor, forced labor, the prevention of HIV/AIDS, and indigenous peoples. At the eighty-sixth International Labour Conference of 1998, the ILO adopted the Declaration on Fundamental Principles and Rights at Work. The declaration asserts that member states will work toward four fundamental principles: freedom of association and collective bargining; discrimination; forced labor; and child labor.

*"The primary goal of the ILO today is to promote opportunities for women and men to obtain decent and productive work, in conditions of freedom, equity, security and human dignity."*
—Juan Somavia, ILO Director-General

| | |
|---|---|
| Past accomplishments | 8/10 |
| International reach | 10/10 |
| Tangibility | 9/10 |
| Peace and hope | 7.5/10 |
| Building a better world | 7/10 |
| | |
| Average score | 8.3/10 |

*Patrick Bonneville: The legacy of Alfred Nobel has helped us build a better world by making us want to be better people, recognized by our peers.*

Alfred Bernhard Nobel was a respected late-nineteenth century chemist, engineer, innovator, and armaments manufacturer from Stockholm, Sweden. He spent his life studying explosives, especially the safe production and use of nitroglycerine, the essential ingredient of dynamite, which he invented.

Along with his inventions, his fortune grew. Upon his death, Alfred Nobel bequeathed an incredible 94 percent of his total assets—the equivalent of $186 million—to a foundation that would award prizes to those who have worked for the betterment of humanity.

The first Nobel Prize was awarded in 1901. The awards honor men and women from all countries and show no prejudice for race, religion, or gender. Since its inception, the foundation has bestowed prizes upon 801 individuals and organizations for their work in five areas: physics, chemistry, medicine, literature, and for building peace.

Each year, invitations are sent to thousands of potential recipients. Once an invitation is received, and the honor of participating is acknowledged, there is a vote and the recipients are announced. Nobel laureates meet for the awards ceremony in Stockholm on December 10 each year, where they receive from King Carl XVI Gustaf of Sweden a Nobel Prize medal, diploma, and a document confirming the cash prize amount they have won.

*"The whole of my remaining realizable estate shall be dealt with in the following way: The capital shall be invested by my executors in safe securities and shall constitute a fund, the interest on which shall be annually distributed in the form of prizes to those who, during the preceding year, shall have conferred the greatest benefit on mankind.*
*—Alfred Nobel, in his will*

**Above:** Alfred Bernhard Nobel
**Right:** The entrance to the Norwegian Nobel Institute in Oslo, Norway

| Past accomplishments | 9.5/10 |
| International reach | 10/10 |
| Tangibility | 3/10 |
| Peace and hope | 9/10 |
| Building a better world | 9.5/10 |
| | |
| Average score | 8.2/10 |

*"Our mission is to influence, encourage and assist societies throughout the world to conserve the integrity and diversity of nature and to ensure that any use of natural resources is equitable and ecologically sustainable."*
—IUCN mission statement

| | |
|---|---|
| Past accomplishments | 9/10 |
| International reach | 9/10 |
| Tangibility | 5/10 |
| Peace and hope | 7.5/10 |
| Building a better world | 10/10 |
| | |
| Average score | 8.1/10 |

*Patrick Bonneville: For a long time I dreamed of working for the IUCN. It is the top organization in species conservation. It monitors how Mother Earth is doing and proposes actions we all can take to save humanity's greatest treasure: nature.*

Founded in 1948, at the prompting of UNESCO, the International Union for the Conservation of Nature and Natural Resources (IUCN) was the world's first global environmental organization. It has also grown to become the world's largest conservation network.

Based in the Lake Geneva area of Switzerland, the IUCN groups together about 10,000 experts and scientists from around the world along with an impressive list of participants: 83 states, 108 government agencies, 766 non-governmental organizations, and 81 international organizations.

These parties are involved in thousands of field projects and conservation activities, such as research and conservation efforts for species, ecosystems, biodiversity, and their impact on human life. The IUCN helps implement laws, policies, and best-practices through a variety of measures. They are also concerned with helping people find sustainable livelihoods that do not compromise the ecosystems they inhabit.

The IUCN englobes six scientific commissions with specific objectives, including education and communication, promoting environmental policies, advancing environmental law worldwide, guiding the management of our ecosystems, working for the survival of threatened species and, finally, the establishment and monitoring of protected areas.

One of the IUCN's best-known major services is the Red List, a vital program that classifies the threatened species of our planet according to their proximity to extinction. It has also contributed to the conservation movement its categories of protected area management, under the auspices of the World Commission on Protected Areas. This program has developed the following classifications: classified nature reserves, wilderness areas, national parks, natural monuments, habitat/species management areas, protected landscape/seascapes, and managed-resource protected areas. It also monitors all World Heritage natural sites.

The IUCN prides itself on being an international organization that crosses cultural barriers and that is well respected for its corporate integrity and ethical behaviour. We are proud that they have a long-term vision for the preservation of the ecosystems that sustain the species that are, for the most part, threatened by the human presence on earth.

**Left:** The vision of IUCN is simply a world that values and conserves nature.

*Patrick Bonneville: It is somewhat comforting to have a UN agency specialized in monitoring the use of atomic energy. We believe the International Atomic Energy Agency makes our world a much a safer place.*

The use of nuclear energy has stirred up much emotion and led to a few political entanglements since the splitting of the atom in 1917. The International Atomic Energy Agency (IAEA) was created in 1957 to ensure the safe and peaceful use of nuclear energy. It is independent of the United Nations but reports to the UN General Assembly and Security Council. With headquarters in Vienna, Austria, the IAEA also has two regional offices: one in Toronto, Canada and the other in Tokyo, Japan. Its laboratories can be found in Austria, Monaco, and Italy.

The purpose of the agency was to put to rest fears of this controversial technology and to prove to critics that nuclear energy was practical, useful, and could be used peacefully. Efforts were made internationally to create legally binding commitments between nations that would outline safeguards to stop the spread of nuclear weapons. The result was the approval of the 1970 Treaty on the Non-Proliferation of Nuclear Weapons, an agreement that includes a moratorium on the number of declared weapons held by the five major nuclear weapon states: the United States, Russia, the United Kingdom, France, and China. The IAEA also oversees the use of such weapons by illegitimate nations, or those not part of the treaty.

The IAEA contributes to the understanding and applications of nuclear energy with a strong team of about 2,200 professionals in over 90 countries. Over one-third of the agency's $4 million budget goes to international peace and security concerns related to nuclear energy.

The efficiency of the IAEA is not without debate; an important example of this was the discovery of Iraq's illegal weapons program in 1991, of which the IAEA had previously been unaware. Nuclear accidents, such as the Three Mile Island meltdown and the Chernobyl disaster, and illicit nuclear developments in Iran and North Korea have also raised doubts about the IAEA's ability to adequately monitor the use of this technology. Nevertheless, the IAEA is the only existing and widely respected moderator that compels all nations to limit their use of nuclear energy for military purposes.

*"Since the Chernobyl accident, we have worked all over the globe to raise nuclear safety performance. And since the September 2001 terrorist attacks, we have worked with even greater intensity on nuclear security."*
—*IAEA Director General Dr. Mohamed ElBaradei, accepting the 2005 Nobel Peace Prize*

**Right:** Cooling towers of a nuclear power plant with steam escaping toward the sky. Cooling towers extract waste heat to the atmosphere.

| Past accomplishments | 10/10 |
| International reach | 9.5/10 |
| Tangibility | 3/10 |
| Peace and hope | 9/10 |
| Building a better world | 9/10 |
| | |
| Average score | 8.1/10 |

*Patrick Bonneville: One could easily argue that OXFAM is the ultimate organization working today to eradicate poverty.*

OXFAM began in 1942 in England with the formation of the Oxford Committee for Famine Relief. Initially, it was a group of Quakers who assembled to campaign for aid for Greek women and children suffering from Allied naval blockades.

Eventually OXFAM spread to over a dozen countries, and its mandate grew to include strategies to eliminate the causes of poverty and famine. OXFAM shops in many of these countries offered goods fairly traded with local producers. The first overseas office was founded in Canada in 1963, where funds are raised today through events such as the Miles for Millions fundraising walks. In 1995, OXFAM International was created to unite national OXFAM groups that remain autonomous. Collectively, the federation raises over $350 million annually. It is registered as a charity in Netherlands and has its headquarters in Oxford, England.

The money raised by OXFAM International is attributed to projects targeting three major areas: development and humanitarian work, as well as lobbying, advocacy, and popular campaigning. Development work focuses on alleviating poverty and creating opportunities for villages and their residents to find sustainable ways of life. And while OXFAM addresses these long-term goals, its humanitarian work brings relief to people in more immediate need, such as in natural or man-made disasters, including war. In order for OXFAM to achieve the first two goals, however, much lobbying and advocacy is required. They campaign for life-improving changes on the international scene by challenging law and policy in specific arenas: agriculture, climate change, trade and economic justice, health and education and, finally, arms control.

*"I had two words—rage and passion. Rage because of the inequality and injustice in the world, and a passion to do something about it."*
*—Joe "The Salesman on the Side of the Angels" Mitty, founder of the OXFAM charity shop*

| | |
|---|---|
| Past accomplishments | 8.5/10 |
| International reach | 8.5/10 |
| Tangibility | 9/10 |
| Peace and hope | 7/10 |
| Building a better world | 7.5/10 |
| Average score | 8.1/10 |

**Left:** Oxfam aid worker Janna Hamilton attends to the wounds of Sio Lauvao in Samoa.
**Right:** Oxfam America youth workshop.

"A joint declaration was issued recognizing the necessity of establishing at the earliest practicable date a general international organization, based on the principle of the sovereign equality of all peace-loving States, and open to membership by all such States, large and small, for the maintenance of international peace and security."
—The International Court of Justice

May Peace Prevail On Earth

*Patrick Bonneville: Nuclear tests. Border disputes. Maritime zones. Wars. Genocides. This court serves us all by carrying out justice for all nations against tyrants.*

**Left:** International Court of Justice in The Hague, Holland.
**Above:** Public hearings at the ICJ.

Also known as the World Court, the International Court of Justice (ICJ) was created in June 1945, by Charter of the United Nations, to resolve interstate disputes. Since its inception, the court has ruled on 93 cases, some of which have involved the use of nuclear arms, genocide, territorial conflicts, fisheries, loans, and many other matters of international law. It is the principal judicial branch of the UN and is the only major branch of the UN headquartered outside the United States; it is located in the Peace Palace, The Hague, Netherlands.

The ICJ is humanity's highest authority on international legal questions. It studies and settles conflicts of law brought to the court by sovereign states and provides non-binding advisory opinions on legal questions submitted by specific United Nations organs and agencies. It does not try individuals. Fifteen judges from different states are elected by the United Nations General Assembly and the Security Council to serve terms of nine years.

| | | |
|---|---|---|
| Past accomplishments | 8/10 | |
| International reach | 8/10 | |
| Tangibility | 7/10 | |
| Peace and hope | 8/10 | |
| Building a better world | 9/10 | |
| | | |
| Average score | 8.0/10 | |

The World Court has issued advisory opinions on such matters as Israel's separation wall in the Palestine territories, which the ICJ deemed as illegal in its entirety, and on the legality of the use of nuclear weapons by states in conflict. It has handed down judgments regarding conflicts between states from the former Yugoslav republic and against the United States for its role in supporting Contra guerillas in the 1980s.

Twice in its history, states have refused to comply with ICJ rulings: in 1984, when the United States refused to comply with the court's ruling for its doings in Nicaragua, and in 1977, when Argentina refused to concede possession of islands in the Beagle Channel to Chile. Since all judgments are final, when a state fails to comply with a ruling, the other state may bring the matter to the Security Council for further resolution. If the complaint is vetoed at the Council, the issue may remain unresolved indefinitely.

*"I fear the newspapers more than a hundred thousand bayonets."*
*—Napoleon Bonaparte*

*Patrick Bonneville: Freedom of speech and access to information are basic rights for everyone. This organization works to ensure that every state knows it.*

Founded in 1985 by Robert Ménard, Rony Braumand, and Jean-Claude Guillebaud, Reporters Without Borders (RWB) has come to be a symbol for freedom of the press. This international organization is based in Paris but works around the world to defend and advocate for journalists and media assistants who are imprisoned, threatnened, or persecuted because of their work.

Originally geared toward promoting the alternative press, the non-profit organization was eventually left in the hands of Ménard, who steered it towards free-press advocacy. Today, RWB strives to fight censorship, expose the exploitation and torture of journalists, and lobby against laws that lead to the erosion of press freedom.

While about 12 percent of its funding comes from governmental organizations, Reporters Without Borders mostly relies on donations from the private sector and on the proceeds from sales of its photo reportage books. Recently, RWB published a guide for bloggers intended to help them avoid censorship and personal persecution.

**Right:** Reporters Without Borders staged a ceremony at the Trocadero human rights plaza in Paris to mark the first anniversary of Russian reporter Anna Politkovskaya's murder in Moscow. **Opposite page:** French advertising campaing.

RWB also publishes the Worldwide Press Freedom Index on its website, rsf.org. This is a ranking of countries based on how they respect press freedom, as evaluated by journalists and other members of the media. In 2009, Denmark, Finland, and Ireland take the top three places, while Eritrea, in northeast Africa, and North Korea are last out of a list of 173 states. France, the home of RWB, was ranked forty-third, the United States was twenty-second, and Canada was nineteenth. The RWB also maintains the Predators of Press Freedom, a list that names individual political leaders whose regimes smother free press initiatives.

*"Violence, arrests, pressures, tailing and threats are the daily lot of the foreign correspondent."*
*—Rober Ménard, founder of Reporters Without Borders.*

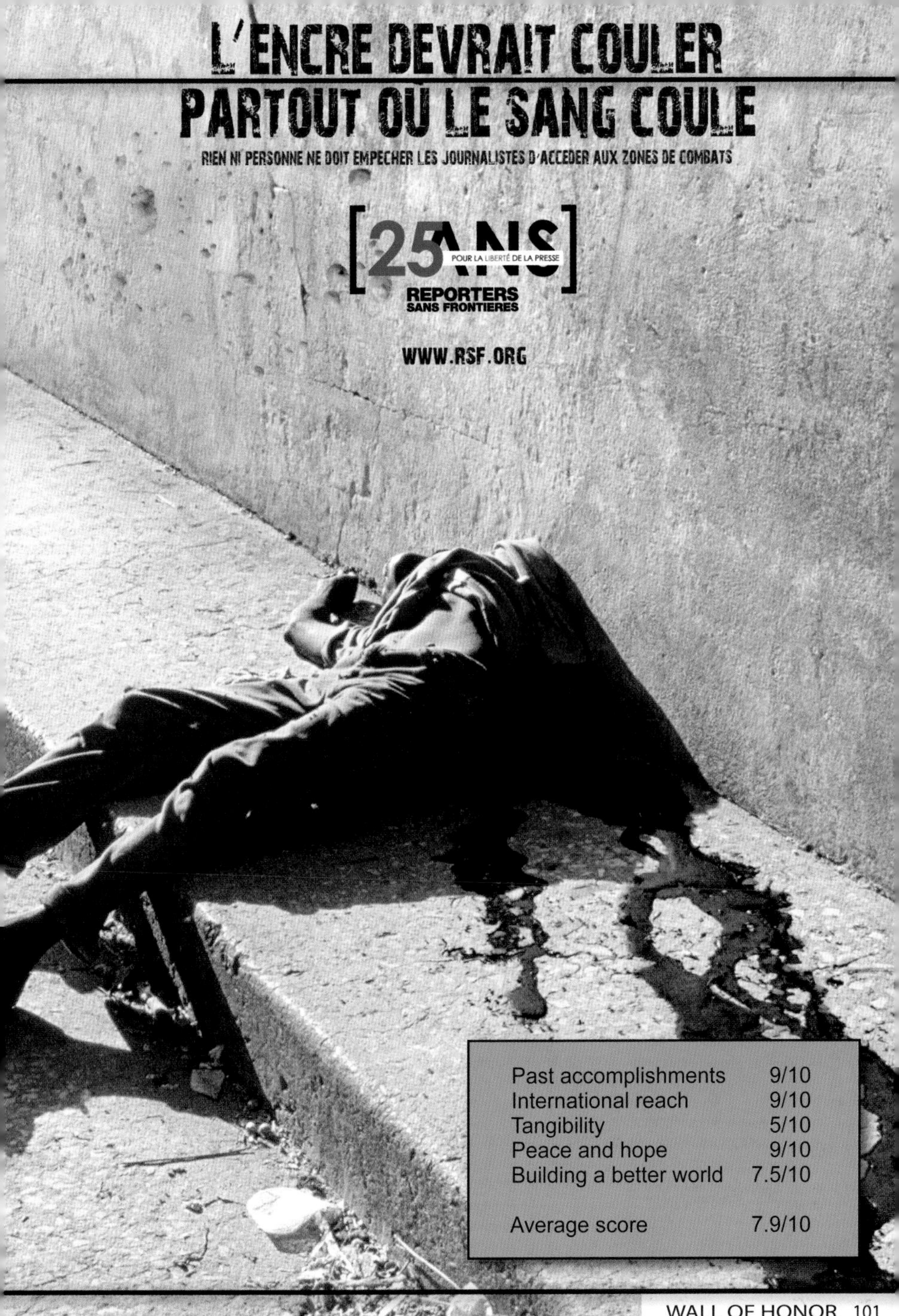

L'ENCRE DEVRAIT COULER
PARTOUT OÙ LE SANG COULE

RIEN NI PERSONNE NE DOIT EMPECHER LES JOURNALISTES D'ACCEDER AUX ZONES DE COMBATS

[25ANS]
POUR LA LIBERTÉ DE LA PRESSE
REPORTERS
SANS FRONTIERES

WWW.RSF.ORG

| | |
|---|---|
| Past accomplishments | 9/10 |
| International reach | 9/10 |
| Tangibility | 5/10 |
| Peace and hope | 9/10 |
| Building a better world | 7.5/10 |
| | |
| Average score | 7.9/10 |

| Past accomplishments | 9/10 |
| International reach | 7/10 |
| Tangibility | 8/10 |
| Peace and hope | 8/10 |
| Building a better world | 7.5/10 |
| | |
| Average score | 7.9/10 |

*Kimberly Murray: At the Global Village and Discovery Center in Americus, Georgia, visitors can walk through constructions that are examples of real living conditions from around the world. A tour can also be taken of replicated Habitat homes that have been built using local materials in various countries.*

To watch a Habitat home be built by volunteers alongside the family who will own it is to understand the capacity for generosity and compassion that humanity embodies. Habitat for Humanity International (HFHI) believes that housing is a fundamental right for all people, and can be achieved in part by providing low-cost materials, knowledge, and logistical support to families in need.

HFHI's beginnings unfolded in Americus, Georgia, in 1976, with founders Millard and Linda Fuller and co-founder Donald Mosley. Through a local project building homes for low-income families, they realized the tremendous life-affirming potential that home building and owning offered to people in need of housing around the world.

**Left:** Women make up half of Habitat's force.
**Above:** Newly constructed house by UN-HABITAT.

The ecumenical non-profit organization they developed into Habitat for Humanity relies on volunteer labor to build the houses that have been sold at no profit in more than 100 countries worldwide, for people of varying ethnicities and religions. Each chapter of Habitat for Humanity is locally run and each management division chooses families according to qualifying criteria.

Today, more than 300,000 homes have been built by more than one million volunteers worldwide from donations and the interest gained from Habitat mortgages. The organization's most famous supporter is former American President Jimmy Carter, who has been involved in fundraising and homebuilding since 1984. In 1996, then-President Bill Clinton awarded Millard Fuller the Presidential Medal of Freedom, the highest civilian honor in the U.S.A. The Fullers are also recipients of more than fifty honorary degrees.

Homes are built in places of need, including in regions hit hard by natural disasters. The homes are not donated; rather, they are sold at cost to low-income families who must contribute 500 hours of their time to the project. Owners must acquire a mortgage and provide a down payment. House prices vary depending on their location — in a developing country, a Habitat house may be valued at about $800, while in the U.S.A. an average house would be mortaged for about $60,000. Mortgage payments are reinvested into the organization so that more homes can be built.

*Patrick Bonneville: The International Crisis Group gathers the most talented and experienced team possible for the resolution of international conflict. The organization is very highly regarded by other NGOs, by the UN, and by the press.*

The ICG was formed in 1995 as a completely independent organization that would work to prevent and resolve violent conflict in the world. It was founded by former journalist and United Nations Deputy Secretary General, Lord Mark Malloch Brown, by American diplomat Morton Abramowitz, and by its first chairman, Senator George Mitchell. Their motivation to found a crisis group arose as the Western world failed to rally resolutions for the disastrous conflicts of the early 1990s in Somalia, Bosnia, and Rwanda.

The small group rapidly grew to include four advocacy offices, including their headquarters in Brussels; Washington DC, New York, and London. It also has liaison staff in Moscow and Beijing. The group has regional representation in twenty-seven other cities, from where analyses and reports are brought to bear on more than sixty-six countries.

As a sort of watch-dog for peace, the ICG analyzes the potential for deadly conflicts around the world and issues warning reports that may allow contentious situations to be avoided or moderated. The group also offers advice to intergovernmental bodies, such as the United Nations, European Union, and

**Above:** Louise Arbour, former UN High Commissioner for Human Rights, is the President and CEO of the International Crisis Group.

the World Bank. Statistically speaking, this group is very active: over 60 conflict and potential conflict situations are covered, over 80 reports and briefings published annually, and over 130,000 people are subscribed online to receive reports.

The ICG employs about 130 people and operates with an annual budget of about $15.5 million. Its employees come from a broad variety of backgrounds and speak 53 different languages. The organization is staffed by many individuals who have considerable respect and influence in the international community.

| Past accomplishments | 6/10 |
| International reach | 9/10 |
| Tangibility | 5.5/10 |
| Peace and hope | 9.5/10 |
| Building a better world | 9.5/10 |
| | |
| Average score | 7.9/10 |

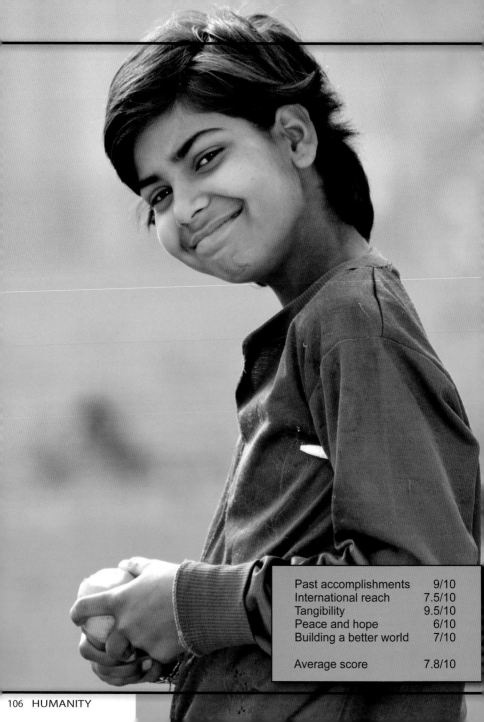

| Past accomplishments | 9/10 |
| International reach | 7.5/10 |
| Tangibility | 9.5/10 |
| Peace and hope | 6/10 |
| Building a better world | 7/10 |
| | |
| Average score | 7.8/10 |

**Opposite page:** Child supported by CARE.
**Left:** Distribution of 200,000 CARE packages in West Berlin, May 12, 1949.
**Below:** Members of the CARE team in Darfur.

In 1945, Arthur Ringland was looking for a way to fund the assembly and shipping of care packages for survivors of World War II overseas. Lincoln Clark and Wallace Campbell joined their talents to Ringland's and created the Cooperative for American Remittances to Europe, which later became the Cooperative for Assistance and Relief Everywhere. Their initial plan was to sell surplus U.S. Army food packages at the cost of $10 each and ship them to the buyer's friends or family in Europe within a reasonable time limit. It was a way to guarantee Americans that their aid was reaching their relatives. It was apparent to the founders that people abroad needed more care. Soon, donations of food and supplies allowed for the creation of custom packages to be shipped to specific areas. CARE needed to have local teams ready to receive and distribute aid.

Today, CARE has grown into one of the largest humanitarian organizations in the world. It currently has programs in over 70 countries and employs more than 12,000 people. While its current mission has evolved to focus on issues that lead to poverty, one of its primary concerns remains the delivery of immediate emergency relief during and after disasters. CARE also campaigns for human rights, access to adequate health and social services for women and people with AIDS, as well as for education and economic development.

Often first on the scene of a natural disaster, CARE remains on the ground long after the initial need passes in order to help develop programs that will allow the community to thrive and heal. Even though the actual CARE packages are long phased out, the idea of the CARE package—the compassion and help these packages represent—remains at the heart of all of CARE's actions.

*"Every CARE Package is a personal contribution to the world peace our nation seeks. It expresses America's concern and friendship in a language all peoples understand."*
*—President John F. Kennedy, 1962*

*Patrick Bonneville: Philanthropists have the potential to improve the world. Their private foundations, such as Bill and Melinda Gates', play a crucial role in our world today.*

Aprivate foundation is a legal entity set up by a single person, a group of people, or a family for a purpose such as philanthropy. Unlike charitable foundations, private ones do not solicit funds from the public. Bill and Melinda Gates' is one such private foundation; its primary goals are to "increase opportunity and equity for those most in need," based on the belief that "every life has equal value." In the U.S.A., the organization is focused on expanding educational opportunities and access to information technology.

Founded in 1994 as the William H. Gates Foundation with an initial endowment of $94 million, it was renamed the Bill & Melinda Gates Foundation in 1999. Bill Gates, ranked as one of the world's richest businessmen, made his fortune as the founder and main shareholder of the software company Microsoft. Currently, his and his wife's Seattle-based institution manages about $2 billion and employs about 700 people.

Notably, the Gates Foundation donated $750 million in 2005 to the Global Alliance for Vaccines and Immunization and has donated a grand total of $287 million to various HIV/AIDS researchers. The HIV/AIDS research money was split between sixteen different

**Right:** A child is administered oral drops as part of the polio immunization drive in India.

teams across the world, on the condition that they share their findings with one another.

The Gates Foundation has also partnered with the Rockefeller Foundation to enhance agricultural science and small-farm productivity in Africa, which builds on the Green Revolution which the Rockefeller Foundation spurred in the 1940s and 1960s. The Gates Foundation has made an initial $100 million investment in this effort, to which the Rockefeller foundation has contributed an additional $50 million.

Each year, the foundation makes an award of up to $1 million to an American public library or similar organization outside the United States that offers an innovative program to provide free access to information technology to the public.

*"These investments are high-risk and high-reward. But the reward isn't measured by financial gain, it's measured by the number of lives saved or people lifted out of poverty."*
*—Bill Gates, describing his investment in his foundation*

| | |
|---|---|
| Past accomplishments | 8/10 |
| International reach | 6/10 |
| Tangibility | 8/10 |
| Peace and hope | 9/10 |
| Building a better world | 8/10 |
| Average score | 7.8/10 |

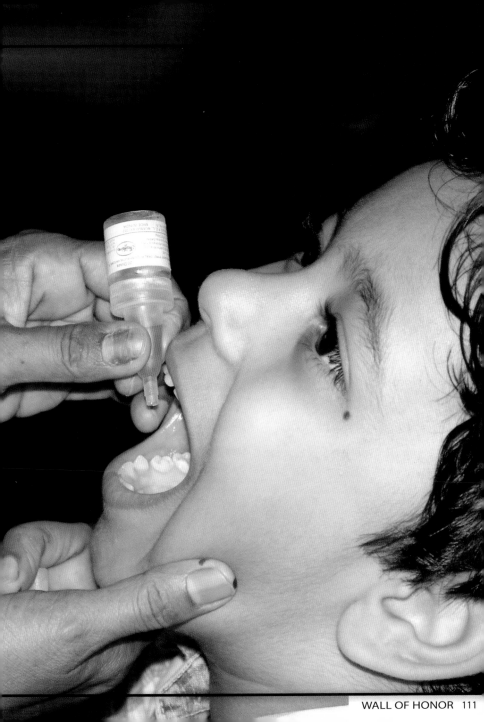

| | |
|---|---|
| Past accomplishments | 8/10 |
| International reach | 7.5/10 |
| Tangibility | 6/10 |
| Peace and hope | 9.5/10 |
| Building a better world | 8/10 |
| | |
| Average score | 7.8/10 |

In recent human history, Europe has become the proof that peace can prevail where once there was tension and hatred. The European Union (EU) is an entity that economically and politically unites twenty-seven states. The union was created in November 1993, when the Treaty of Maastricht extended the principles that had previously united European states under the name European Communities. Its approximately 730 million citizens, from eighty-seven distinct cultural groups, have the right to travel, work, and live anywhere in the Union. They have the right to a European health insurance card, which can help cover medical costs should a citizen fall ill in another European country, and they also are guaranteed the recognition of higher education qualifications with certain conditions.

The road to this union of states took a long time to build. After World War II, integration was believed by many to be a way of escape from the extreme forms of nationalism that resulted in war. In 1967, the European Coal and Steel Community, the European Economic Community, and the European Atomic Energy Community merged and became known collectively as the European Communities, or more commonly, the European Community (EC).

The fall of the Iron Curtain was a defining event for the the EC. When, in 1990, East Germany reunited with West Germany, the economic benefits of a formal European union were clear.

**Left:** Paris celebrating the European Union.

In Nice, France, in 2000, the Charter of Fundamental Rights of the European Union was signed; in it are fifty-four articles detailing the fundamental values and the civil, political, economic, and social rights of all EU citizens. They include rights concerning family life, professional life, healthcare, social security, and social assistance. The Charter is progressive in certain aspects, such as the reproductive cloning of humans, environmental protection, and freedom from fear of persecution or violence.

With the freedom of movement guaranteed by the Union came the opportunity for the exploitation of these rights. Extra security measures were needed at the EU's external borders, and within the EU, national police forces and judicial authorities are required to work together more efficiently to address cross-border issues and crime. The application process for immigration is also scheduled to become harmonized. Applicants for asylum are treated according to a basic set of principles that gives equal status throughout the Union. Such a complicated process implies a greater need for cooperative policing and legal systems.

Policies for cross-border freedom grew from 1985's Schengen Agreement between five states—Belgium, France, Germany, Luxembourg and the Netherlands—to include almost all EU members today. And while some members have not signed the agreement, some non-EU countries such as Iceland and Norway have agreed to fully apply the rules.

*Patrick Bonneville: Part of Western cultural lore, the Salvation Army's statistics speak for themselves: 115 countries, 1,603 charity shops, and about 108,000 employees.*

A look at the origins of the Salvation Army takes us back to the mid-1800s in London, England, when Methodist minister William Booth felt summoned to full-time evangelism. He and his wife Catherine were invited to join a Christian group that preached in the streets, and soon he was leading the East London Christian Mission. Booth worked on the streets and Catherine worked among the rich to solicit financial contributions that would enable their mission work to continue.

When his son insisted on being called a "regular" rather than a volunteer, Booth conceived the idea of evangelizing as a quasi-army—the Salvation Army. Members adopted a military-style uniform and used military expressions for aspects of worship, administration, and practice. Initially, members playing musical instruments accompanied evangelists in the streets to distract negative attention from the missionaries. Eventually, however, they became a central aspect of the Salvation Army's identity, and today some churches enjoy the music of professional-quality brass bands.

Colloquially called the Sally Ann in North America, the Sally Army in the United Kingdom, and the Salvos in Australia, today, the Salvation Army still acts according to the principle attributed to William Booth: soup, soap, and salvation. While the Salvation Army's objectives are expressly to communicate its Christian beliefs to people in need, the charity's social interventions are among the most respected in the Western world; its outreach extends to well over 110 countries, where its remedies to poverty are adapted to match the language and culture of the place in question.

*"We are a salvation people—this is our speciality—getting saved and keeping saved, and then getting somebody else saved, and then getting saved ourselves more and more until full salvation on earth makes the heaven within, which is finally perfected by the full salvation without, on the other side of the river."*
*—Salvation Army first general, William Booth*

| Past accomplishments | 8/10 |
| International reach | 7/10 |
| Tangibility | 9.5/10 |
| Peace and hope | 7/10 |
| Building a better world | 7/10 |
| | |
| Average score | 7.7/10 |

*Patrick Bonneville: This Christian relief organization has a huge presence in the media. It appears on TV and in magazines, making sure that we know about the little ones they serve.*

In 1951, Dr. Robert Pierce, a pastor and missionary, began sending five dollars a month to support a Chinese girl whom he'd met while on a mission trip. This was the seed of World Vision (WV), an international children's relief organization that provides each sponsor-donor with a photo and profile of a child in a community receiving WV aid. World Vision's mission is to follow God's will by working with the poor to bring them social justice, transformation, and exposure to the Gospels.

Through fundraising from the private sector as well as from multilateral aid organizations, World Vision International is a federation of national WV groups who are relatively autonomous in their decision-making. International headquarters are located in Federal Way, Washington; however there are partnership offices in Geneva, Bangkok, Nairobi, Cyprus, Los Angeles, and San José, Costa Rica. The organization maintains an on-the-ground presence in ninety-seven countries.

World Vision's mission is driven by a variety of strategies, which include providing emergency relief, education, health care, economic development, and promotion of justice. While many sponsor-donors have the impression that their financial contribution is alloted directly to a child and her family, the organization in fact takes what it calls "a community-based approach." This means that funds are applied to projects that serve to improve access to education for all of the children in a community, as well as to nutritious food, clothing, health care, agricultural assistance, and medicine. WV also funds evangelical activities around the world and provides leadership training for what it identifies as Christian leaders in local communities.

**Upper right:** School children in London, June 5, 2009, launching World Vision's Week for Children.
**Right:** World Vision distributes rice to families devastated by the Haiti 2010 earthquake.
**Opposite page:** World Vision sponsored child in Mozambique.

| Past accomplishments | 8/10 |
| --- | --- |
| International reach | 7/10 |
| Tangibility | 8.5/10 |
| Peace and hope | 7/10 |
| Building a better world | 8/10 |
| | |
| Average score | 7.7/10 |

*Patrick Bonneville: It is very important for the rest of the world that these leaders meet regularly to ensure global security and stability.*

The Group of Twenty (G-20) is a forum for Central Bank governors and finance ministers from the world's twenty most powerful economies. Collectively, its members make up 85 percent of the global gross national product, 80 percent of world trade, and two-thirds of the world's population. The organization's goal is to study and review policies that concern the players in the global marketplace as well as discuss international financial stability. Recently, its leaders announced that the G-20 will replace the G-8 group as the world's principal council of powerful economies.

The organization was formed as a result of financial turbulence in 1997-1999 and superceded earlier international forums of the world's wealthiest nations. Its first meeting was held in 1999 in Berlin, and subsequent meetings have been held bi-annually. G-20 summits have centered around themes such as

**Below:** G20 leaders, Washington, DC, 2008.
**Right:** G20 meetings are opportunities for its members to work together.

building and maintaining prosperity, global energy, reform of the International Monetary Fund and the World Bank, and solutions for economic depression.

Members of the G-20 are: Argentina, Australia, Brazil, Canada, the People's Republic of China, France, Germany, India, Indonesia, Italy, Japan, Mexico, Republic of Korea, Russia, Saudi Arabia, South Africa, Turkey, the United Kingdom, the United States of America, the European Union, the World Bank, the International Monetary Fund, and the Financial Stability Forum. Because of the group's size, informal exchange is encouraged among members.

Critics of the G-20 advance that while it represents a significant portion of the world's finances, the group omits the voices of the world's other 170 governments in its discussions of global scope. Many people feel the G-20 is, in practice, a forum for the advancement of the leading nations at the price of those not represented there.

| Past accomplishments | 8.5/10 |
| International reach | 8.5/10 |
| Tangibility | 5/10 |
| Peace and hope | 7.5/10 |
| Building a better world | 9/10 |
| | |
| Average score | 7.7/10 |

*Patrick Bonneville: Cancer is a trial that awaits many of us. Scientists from all over the world are trying to find cures for this global threat that takes so many forms. They must all work together to win that race.*

It might be said that there is not a single person on earth whose life has not been touched in some way by cancer. The International Union Against Cancer, or *Union Internationale Contre le Cancer* (UICC), is an international non-governmental organization whose mission is to fight cancer worldwide. Based in Geneva, Switzerland, the UICC consists of over 280 organizations from more than 90 countries working to create a cancer-free world.

According to the American Cancer Society, 7.6 million people die every year from the disease. In 2005, cancer claimed twice as many lives as did AIDS. It is on the rise in developing nations, where costly treatments are not accessible to all people.

The term "cancer" is a generic term that groups together diseases that have similar characteristics. In cancer diseases, cells mutate and act differently from "normal" cells. Cancer can be linked to diet, phyisical activity, and cultural behaviors, such as smoking. It can also occur as a consequence of other ailments such as hepatitis B, which causes liver cancer, and the human papilloma virus, which causes cervical cancer. There are also environmental causes for many types of cancer. Early diagnosis and treatment is the key to survival. Western societies have taken important strides in communicating this message, especially concerning cervical and breast cancers; in developing nations, there is no such progess. Cancer has thus become an urgent humanitarian crisis.

The UICC supports activities that are based on scientic evidence. The organization has no commercial or political interests, focusing instead on internationally revelant projects and equality in treatment for all people. It works in concert with the World Health Organization, the International Agency for Reseach on Cancer, and the Programme of Action for Cancer Therapy, which gather to discuss and debate key cancer issues and share strategies.

Some of the UICC's specific initiatives focus on the sharing and transfer of information and technology. Communication campaigns, such as World Cancer Day and the My Child Matters project, which has funded projects in several developing countries, have been successful in increasing awareness in the international community about the severity of cancer and the importance of early detection. The UICC is also strongly involved in creating a tobacco-free world in which the incidence of cancer would drop significantly.

**Right:** Breast cancer represents 10% of all new cancers diagnosed per year.

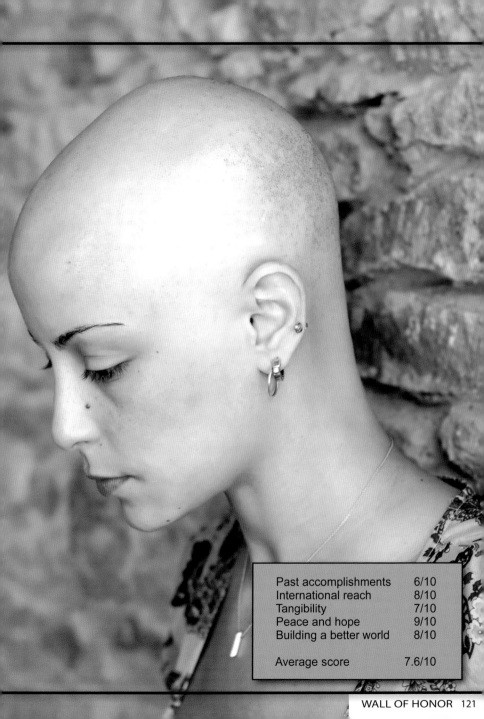

| Past accomplishments | 6/10 |
| International reach | 8/10 |
| Tangibility | 7/10 |
| Peace and hope | 9/10 |
| Building a better world | 8/10 |
| | |
| Average score | 7.6/10 |

A central cog in the engine of worldwide sustainable development, the United Nations Environment Programme (UNEP) works to develop environmental policies that will ensure the planet's resources last for future generations. The organization assists developing countries in implementing such practices. Headquartered in Nairobi, Kenya, there are six regional offices worldwide.

UNEP was launched after the UN hosted the first international conference on environmental issues in Stockholm, Sweden, in 1972. At the Stockholm Conference, policy makers, governments, and NGOS began to agree that economic development and the environment are inextricably linked. Without a healthy environment, development will certainly fail. That conference saw the launch of a number of research projects designed to educate and illuminate governments on the critical issues facing the environment. These initiatives led to successful legislation in many parts of the world.

Seven adminstrative branches oversee UNEP work: Early Warning and Assessment; Environmental Policy Implementation; Technology, Industry and Economics; Regional Cooperation; Environmental Law and Conventions; Global Environment Facility Coordination; and Communications and Public Information.

**Right:** UNEP played an important role at the 2009 Copenhagen Summit.

Some of UNEP's early initiatives are still inspiring environmentalists today. In 1987, the Montreal Protocol of the Vienna Convention for the Protection of the Ozone Layer was signed. It is considered the most successful summit of international scope, with countries joining long after 1987. Most recently, China signed the agreement in 1999. The Montreal Protocol laid out terms for the reduction and elimination of greenhouse gases so that if all countries enforce the policies, the ozone layer will once again be replenished by 2050. Also in 1987, the World Commission on Environment and Development published *Our Common Future*, a report detailing the concept of sustainable development.

The reach of this organization is broad; today, there are few organizations that do not adhere to some kind of environmental or sustainable policy.

*"To provide leadership and encourage partnership in caring for the environment by inspiring, informing and enabling nations and peoples to improve their quality of life without compromising that of future generations."*
—The UNEP mission

| | |
|---|---|
| Past accomplishments | 7/10 |
| International reach | 10/10 |
| Tangibility | 4/10 |
| Peace and hope | 8/10 |
| Building a better world | 9/10 |
| Average score | 7.6/10 |

COP15
COPENHAGEN
UNITED NATIONS CLIMATE CHANGE CONFERENCE 2009

"We don't know when. We don't know where. But let us not forget that each seed that we have stored inside that seed vault has the potential to do just that—to save the world."
—Norwegian Minister of Agriculture and Food Lars Peder Brekk

Deep in the permafrost of the mountains of Svalbard, Norway, is a vault containing something many consider more valuable than gold, diamonds, or oil. The precious collection is seeds: something so vital to humanity that a secure, temperature controlled environment was created specifically for its protection. Sometimes called the "Doomsday Seed Vault," it is a remote and mostly unstaffed conservation facility that holds some 2.25 billion seeds from around the world. Its purpose is to protect them and ensure that the diversity of the world's food seeds are preserved for posterity.

The Svalbard Global Seed Vault is financed by the Norwegian government's ministry of foreign affairs, ministry of environment, and ministry of agriculture and food. The government provides the storage for free to those who have seeds considered important to humanity, with priority given to seeds that are sources of food and sustainable agriculture. Individuals and organizations wishing to store such seeds may submit a request for storage to the vault.

The vault's underground chambers are kept at a constant temperature of -18°C and can house 4.5 million samples containing 500 seeds each. While it is not the only seed bank in the world, the Svalbard Vault has the storage capacity of all the other 1,400 banks—in 100 countries—combined. The vault is designed to be expandable, should the need arise.

Since it is clearly understood that the loss of plant varieties from environmental change or human interference leads to the loss of animal habitats, it is essential for all the ecosphere that every known plant's seeds eventually be conserved. The vault's seeds can be used to re-introduce native plants to areas devasted by war, natural disasters, or neglect.

Unlike other facilities, the seed vault is not a seed bank. It is a safe-storage service for the preservation of collections on behalf of private or public seed banks. The seeds stored in the vault are intended to be made available only when the original collection cannot be accessed. The depositor retains their rights over the seeds submitted and if a request is made from someone other than the owner, the vault acts as intermediary between the two parties. The seed vault follows strict international regulations under the Multilateral System of the International Treaty on Plant Genetic Resources for Food and Agriculture (ITPGRFA).

The long-term usefulness of the vault is ensured through the periodic regermination of seeds; those whose potential for germination is compromised by age are regularly removed from the vault, planted, and new seeds harvested to replace the originals. Some seeds have a short life span in their frozen state, such as twenty to thirty years. Others can last hundreds of years.

**Right:** Front entrance of the Svalbard Global Seed Vau

| Past accomplishments | 7/10 |
| --- | --- |
| International reach | 9.5/10 |
| Tangibility | 5/10 |
| Peace and hope | 9/10 |
| Building a better world | 7.5/10 |
| Average score | 7.6/10 |

| | |
|---|---|
| Past accomplishments | 8/10 |
| International reach | 8.5/10 |
| Tangibility | 9/10 |
| Peace and hope | 6/10 |
| Building a better world | 6/10 |
| | |
| Average score | 7.5/10 |

Some organizations provide uniquely efficient ways of helping humanity. ORBIS International is a nonprofit NGO that focuses on saving the eyesight of people in underserved areas around the world by working with local professionals and organizations. It is well documented that a lack of proper nutrition and the presence of disease contribute to visual impairment. The World Health Organization estimates that 28 million patients suffer from blindnesses that could have been prevented or treated.

In the 1970s, Dr David Paton, head of ophthalmology at Baylor College of Medicine in Texas, noticed during his travels that there was a lack of training opportunities for doctors and nurses in the field in developing countries. Since 90 percent of blindness occurs in these countries, he set out to find a way to bring new techniques and better services to the professionals helping eye patients.

Dr Paton's solution was a flying teaching hospital that would rely on volunteers—from airline pilots to doctors to faculty members. Eventually, a DC-8 plane was equipped to begin teaching and treating people in developing nations. Since 1982, ORBIS has treated more than 6.8 million patients in 86 countries and has helped more than 195,000 eye care professionals develop their clinical and diagnostic skills.

**Lower left:** The ORBIS Flying Eye Hospital team arriving in Mandalay, Myanmar.
**Right:** Blind in his left eye, Bonsa Lalenda (10) came to ORBIS to save his right eye.

Today, the ORBIS plane contains, at the front, a 48-seat classroom where lectures, discussions, and even live broadcasts of surgical procedures are offered to trainees. The plane is literally a forum where they can see modern techniques, new methods, and exchange information with their peers. The Flying Eye Hospital is also equipped to transport trainees to larger venues, such as a hospital, if required.

Local doctors preselect patients whose particular conditions will be relevant to the education program planned on the Flying Eye Hospital. ORBIS faculty members then screen these patients in order to offer services to the most needy; priority goes to children and individuals who are bilaterally blind and who could not otherwise afford treatment. Local doctors remain active in the patient's care after the intervention.

Along with the World Health Organization, ORBIS created "Vision 2020: The Right to Sight," an ambitious program to eliminate avoidable blindness around the world by the year 2020.

In 1993, two British filmmakers founded War Child, a non-governmental organization, to raise money for aid agencies operating in the former Yugoslavia. Today, War Child continues, bringing basic relief to war-torn regions and psychosocial workshops to children in the form of music therapy.

The support of the business community and of such music industry notables as U2, Avril Lavigne, Coldplay, and Our Lady Peace, allows War Child to pursue its goal of promoting awareness about the problems facing children in war zones and rallying public support for them. War Child's strategy involves developing aid projects and programs, providing funding and logistical support for other NGOs working to the same end, and creating links with the media and entertainment industries in order to publicize the cause.

Artist participation at War Child proves that every human can play a part in the transformation of a child's life. By purchasing a single music CD, funds are directly allocated where they are most needed.

| | | |
|---|---|---|
| Past accomplishments | 7/10 | |
| International reach | 6/10 | |
| Tangibility | 8/10 | |
| Peace and hope | 7.5/10 | |
| Building a better world | 9/10 | |
| | | |
| Average score | 7.5/10 | |

A young organization, War Child quickly established its spot on the Wall of Fame, and will continue to hold on to it.

*"War has everything to do with each and every one of us, no matter where we live in the world; we cannot disengage, and we cannot offer excuses, we are a part of war and so too is it a part of us, and anyone who has not lived the horror of war, or touched it, or been scarred by it should not see that as a reason to disengage; instead, let us see it as an even greater reason to demonstrate the depth of our compassion as human beings. It is not a question of charity; it is a question of our common humanity, and the kind of world we want to live in."*
*—Dr Samantha Nutt, co-founder of War Child Canada*

**Upper left:** Celebrating the organization at the Underage Festival, United Kingdom.
**Below:** Boy and father meeting soldiers in Iraq.

"*These five rings represent the five parts of the world which now are won over to Olympism and willing to accept healthy competition.*"
—*Pierre de Coubertin*

*Patrick Bonneville: Every two years now, countries from around the world meet for a great celebration of athleticism. During the Olympic Games, political agendas are meant to fall by the wayside. Dreams become reality for athletes. Friendships are made. The world celebrates.*

According to the Olympic Charter, the goal of the Olympic movement is to contribute to building a peaceful and better world through sport. This is to be done without discrimination of any kind and in a spirit of mutual understanding, friendship, solidarity, and fair play. The Olympic Games bring together people from all walks of life, from every corner of the globe.

The Baron Pierre de Coubertin, a French historian, founded the International Olympic Committee (IOC) in 1894. He theorized that a cause of France's defeat was because the French soldiers of the Franco-Prussian war had not received adequate physical education. He believed that a large-scale revival of Olympic-style games was possible and would provide a healthy link between sport and education.

**Left:** Chantal Petitclerc won 11 Olympic gold medals.
**Above:** Pierre de Coubertain.
**Right:** 2008 Summer Olympics, Tiananmen Square.

A mere two years later, the first international, multi-lingual Olympic Games were held in Athens Greece. An estimated 80,000 spectators witnessed the historic meeting of athletes, grouped by nation, on the infield.

Today, the IOC is based in Lausanne, Switzerland, from where it ensures the continuity of the Games through supervising and supporting decisions and organizational issues regarding the games, controlling the budget and generating revenue, assuring that rules and regulations are adhered to, and investigating allegations of wrongdoing. The IOC also manages all broadcast partnerships and sponsorships. They distribute approximately 92 percent of marketing revenue to support the Games. The IOC now administrates the bi-annual Winter Games and the Paralympics.

"Olympic ideals are also United Nations ideals: tolerance, equality, fair play and, most of all, peace. Together, the Olympics and the United Nations can be a winning team. But the contest will not be won easily. War, intolerance and deprivation continue to stalk the earth. We must fight back. Just as athletes strive for world records, so must we strive for world peace"
—Kofi A. Annan, United Nations Secretary General, September 2000

| | |
|---|---|
| Past accomplishments | 8/10 |
| International reach | 9/10 |
| Tangibility | 4/10 |
| Peace and hope | 9/10 |
| Building a better world | 7/10 |
| | |
| Average score | 7.4/10 |

*Patrick Bonneville: When this organization has a mandate to arrest an individual, there are not many places to hide—police forces all around the world are alerted and supplied with the information needed to identify and apprehend.*

The International Criminal Police Organization (Interpol) is a cooperative program between nations that ensures international policing. The organization began in 1923 in Austria as the International Criminal Police Commission, and today it is the second-largest intergovernmental organization after the United Nations. Its membership consists of 187 countries, which contribute to Interpol's $59 million annual budget.

Based in Lyon, France, the organization's general secretariat employs some 500 people from nearly eighty different countries. Interpol Red Notices, or transmissions of any national police force's warrant for arrest, lead to about 3,500 arrests per year.

Neutrality is vital: the Interpol constitution prohibits involvement in crimes that do not overlap into several member countries or in crimes of a political, military, religious, or racial nature. Interpol's primary focus is public safety, with a focus on terrorism, organized crime, war crimes, illicit drug production, drug trafficking, weapons smuggling, human trafficking, money laundering, child pornography, white-collar crimes, computer crimes, intellectual property crime, and corruption.

**Above:** INTERPOL Secretary General, American Ronald Kenneth Noble.
**Right:** INTERPOL notices are used by the International Criminal Tribunals and the International Criminal Court to seek persons wanted for genocide, war crimes, and crimes against humanity.

Interpol's database of unsolved crimes and of convicted and alleged criminals is available to any member nation, since information sharing is essential to solving cross-border crime. Its information hub also includes such data as DNA profiles, fingerprints, and stolen property such as passports or vehicles.

Interpol also provides ready support to law enforcement officials in the field. Support is also provided in the form of police training initiatives, advice, and guidance.

| | |
|---|---|
| Past accomplishments | 9/10 |
| International reach | 10/10 |
| Tangibility | 6/10 |
| Peace and hope | 6/10 |
| Building a better world | 6/10 |
| Average score | 7.4/10 |

In 1969, the United Nations Population Fund (UNFPA) was modelled out of the United Nations Fund for Population Activites. The UNFPA works in partnership with other United Nations agencies, governments, and communities to raise awareness about the rights of all people to family planning, safe birthing, freedom from HIV and AIDS, and respect for girls and women.

and assembles the support and resources needed to attain the Millennium Development Goals.

UNFPA is a "hands-on" organization with a large staff presence in the field. Over 140 countries benefit from the agency's programs in four geographic zones: the Arab states and Europe, Asia and the Pacific Rim, Latin America and the Caribbean, and Sub-Saharan Africa. Most UNFPA efforts are focused on reproductive health and sexually transmitted diseases, including HIV/AIDS.

The UNFPA is dedicated to achieving the Millennium Develement Goals set out by the United Nations that require, by 2015, specific increases in universal access to reproductive health services, education, reducing maternal and infant mortality, increasing life expectancy, and reducing HIV infection rates.

*"The main priority of the UNFPA is to prevent women from dying giving birth in Africa, South America and Asia. That is our priority number one."*
*—Abubakar Dungus, UNFPA*

**Above:** Ann Erb-Leoncavallo, Speechwriter in the office of the Executive Director of the UNFPA briefs the media at UN Headquarters in New York.
**Right:** According to the UNFPA, we will be 9 billion by 2050.

*"UNFPA, the United Nations Population Fund, is an international development agency that promotes the right of every woman, man and child to enjoy a life of health and equal opportunity. UNFPA supports countries in using population data for policies and programmes to reduce poverty and to ensure that every pregnancy is wanted, every birth is safe, every young person is free of HIV/AIDS, and every girl and woman is treated with dignity and respect."*
*—The UNFPA mission statement.*

| | |
|---|---|
| Past accomplishments | 7.5/10 |
| International reach | 10/10 |
| Tangibility | 6.5/10 |
| Peace and hope | 6.5/10 |
| Building a better world | 6/10 |
| Average score | 7.3/10 |

**Left:** African Finance Ministers meeting at a World Bank meeting.

As much as it creates controversy, the World Bank also creates hope. Formed at the Bretton Woods Conference in 1944, today, the Bank is dedicated to the achievement of the Millennium Develoment Goals that outline improved living conditions for people in the world's poorest countries.

As their contribution to international development, the World Bank issues low-interest loans to middle-income countries. Investment loans are offered for the support of economic development projects, and quick loans are issued in support of policy and institutional reforms. Requests for loans are examined and evaluated in order to judge the success of the potential project in regards to environmental, economical, financial and social factors.

Countries must show that their projects are innovative and include cooperation with local organizations and stakeholders. Such projects might include debt relief, water and sanitation projects, immunization programs, and environmental programs that will contribute to the development of communities.

The World Bank walks a delicate balance in its function. Its first mandate is that of a political organization that must answer to the demands of the governments, countries, and other international organizations that borrow or make requests from the Bank. On the other hand, it is also an action-oriented organization; in theory they should remain neutral in delivering their aid, assistance, loans, and grants. These roles are often contradictory to each other. Indeed, criticism levelled at the World Bank center around the potential for conflict of interest: the approved loans and grants favor the interests of the countries in charge of the bank, rather than the best interests of the developing nations. Although there are 184 countries with interest in the World Bank, it is governed by a relatively small group of powerful economies.

The World Bank is currently involved in over 1,800 projects, and the financial assistance they have loaned reaches $23.6 billion. The World Bank makes a supreme effort to distribute funds and support policy and programs that are in the best interest of the recipients.

| | |
|---|---|
| Past accomplishments | 8/10 |
| International reach | 10/10 |
| Tangibility | 7/10 |
| Peace and hope | 6.5/10 |
| Building a better world | 5/10 |
| Average score | 7.3/10 |

*Patrick Bonneviolle: "This is the most democratic sport I know. The beauty of it is that any kid in the world can play it. All they need is a ball to dream of taking over the whole world as their heroes do. Or, they can just get away from their daily problems to have fun with their friends."*

The Fédération Internationale de Football Association (FIFA) governs the sport of soccer, or football as it is known outside North America. The organization's mission is to "develop the game, touch the world, build a better future." FIFA takes seriously its responsibility to promote soccer as a symbol of hope and of integration. It works to ensure that the highest level of sportsmanship is maintained on soccer fields around the world, that standards are observed, and that competition is encouraged. Not bound by race, religion, or status, the sport is played from the dusty plains of Africa to the high-tech stadiums of North America.

The World Cup is the FIFA event that brings together the best male teams from the association once every four years to battle for glory. No other sports event—indeed no other television event—is watched more than the World Cup.

FIFA promotes soccer through educational and cultural programs. It believes that the sport must remain authentic to itself and that it remain a simple game available to everyone worldwide. They believe that football should promote solidarity in both the local community and the global community. FIFA also strongly believes that football is a model of fair play, tolerance, and true sportsmanship.

*"Sport is a medium; it is humanity, a way to unite people. On the pitch, everyone is equal and can express themselves freely. The 2010 World Cup will be an opportunity for the world to get to know Africa as a whole, beginning with South Africa."*
*—Romero Britto, Brasilian painter*

**Left:** Italian defender and captain Fabio Cannavaro raises the World Cup trophy after Italy defeated France in Berlin's Olympic Stadium to win the 2006 FIFA World Cup Final.
**Right:** The 2010 FIFA World Cup.

| | |
|---|---|
| Past accomplishments | 8/10 |
| International reach | 9.5/10 |
| Tangibility | 3/10 |
| Peace and hope | 7/10 |
| Building a better world | 9/10 |
| Average score | 7.3/10 |

Since it was first officially documented in 1981, Acquired Immune Deficiency Syndrome (AIDS) has been one of the most devastating epidemics in the history of humanity. It has taken the lives of more than 25 million people worldwide in just under thirty years. AIDS is not prejudiced; its victims include adults and children from all over the world. Nevertheless, more than two-thirds of those afflicted by the disease live in Sub-Saharan African countries.

The Joint United Nations Programme on HIV and AIDS—UNAIDS—researches, campaigns, educates, and coordinates global action on the disease and on HIV, the virus that causes it. Established in 1994, the program's mission is to develop and support strategies to confront HIV and AIDS. According to its Web site, the measures that UNAIDS supports include preventing the transmission of HIV, providing care and support to those already living with the virus, reducing the vulnerability of individuals and communities, and alleviating the impact of the epidemic. UNAIDS also operates a knowledge center, a resource forum for members of the media, practitioners, researchers, policy makers, and advocates.

Funding for AIDS programs has grown to an estimated $10 billion annually, up from about $260 million a little over a decade ago. This dramatic increase is largely due to international funding initiatives. It is vital that proper management of the funds be exercised, with an imperative on distributing funds to areas affected, particularly those in developing nations. Given that there are currently 33.2 million people living with HIV and that 2.5 million new people are diagnosed each year, UNAIDS is playing a central role in one of the most dramatic stories of humanity.

*"(Are we) in for a new wave of virus disease now that the bacterial illnesses are so nearly conquered (?)"*
*—Sir Robert Platt, then-president of the Royal College of Physicians, 1959, writing about what may have been the first case of AIDS in the United Kingdom*

**Left:** Aids educational warning sign in Zambia.
**Above:** Mabathogna High School, Lesotho. Students discuss issues related to sex education.
**Right:** Giant AIDS red ribbon on Paris city hall.

| | |
|---|---|
| Past accomplishments | 7/10 |
| International reach | 8/10 |
| Tangibility | 9/10 |
| Peace and hope | 7/10 |
| Building a better world | 5/10 |
| | |
| Average score | 7.2/10 |

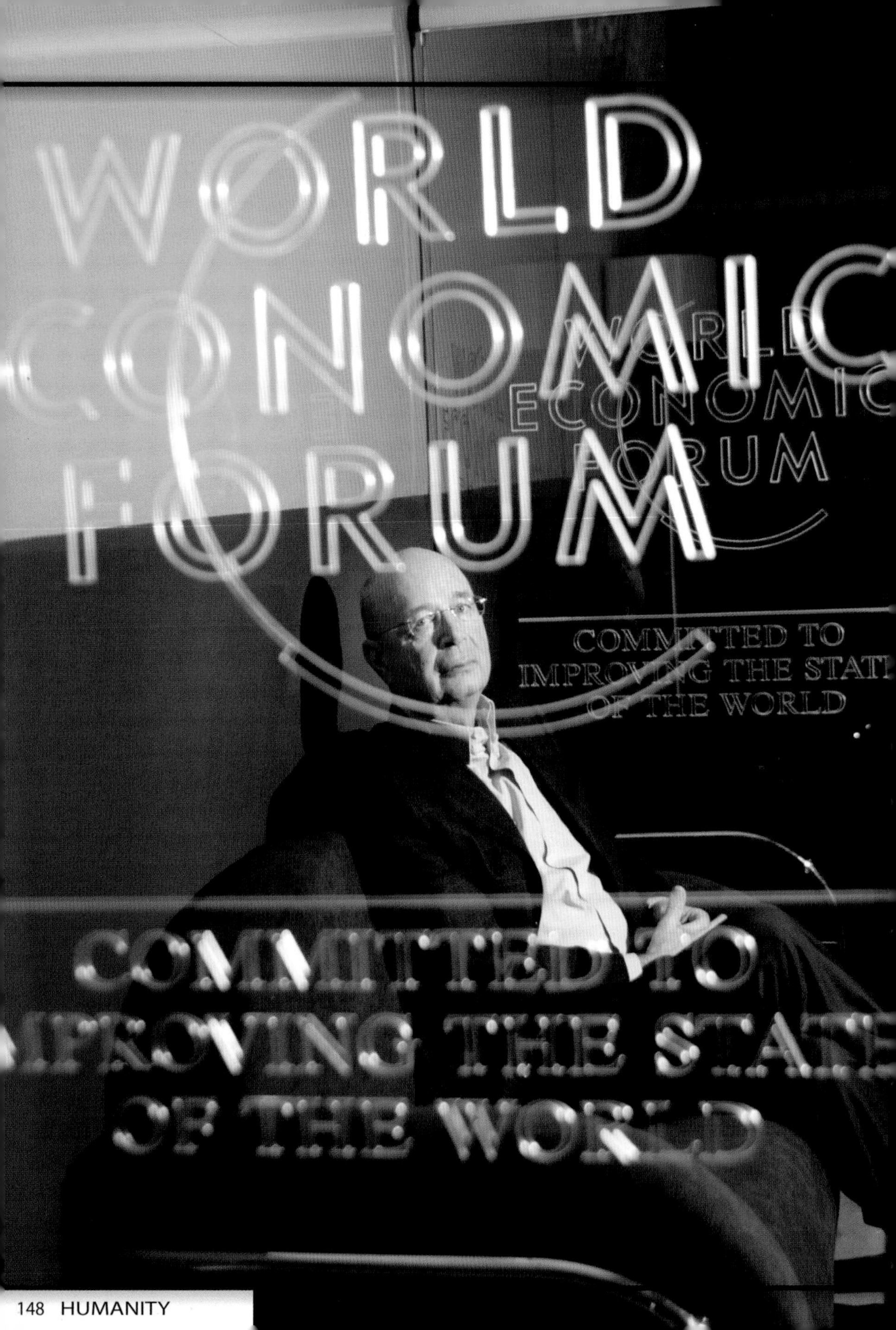
WORLD
FORUM
COMMITTED TO
OF THE WORLD

*Patrick Bonneville: The World Economic Forum aims to facilitate economic cooperation among nations. It has succeeded in brining to the same table, year after year, the international actors who make key decisions that affect economies around the globe.*

**Opposite page:** Klaus Martin Schwab, founder and executive chairman of the World Economic Forum. **Left:** Yasser Arafat shakes hands with Shimon Peres at the World Economic Forum in 2001.

The World Economic Forum was the vision of one particular man, German economist Klaus Martin Schwab. Since its early incarnation in early 1970s, significant achievements have been made in Davos, and not only purely economic. In 1988, for example, representatives of Greece and Turkey signed the "Davos Declaration," thereby avoiding a war between the two countries. In 2000, the creation of the Global Alliance for Vaccines and Immunization (GAVI) was announced in Davos, and at the 2003 forum, a free trade zone between the United States and Arab nations was declared.

A t first sight, Davos seems like a simple, beautiful town located in the Swiss Alps. For a few days each year, the whole world turns its attention to the peaceful alpine town of about 11,000 citizens: politicians, CEOs, and influential NGOs gather there to discuss the state of the world's economy at the World Economic Forum.

Their discussions are not about profits, corporate margins, or investment returns. They are genuine open-ended discussions about global economic stability and the issues that influence it. The organization purports to work for the global public interest: the women and men behind the World Economic Forum believe global social development leads to global economic progress. This explains the strong presence of NGOs from all around the world at this important meeting.

Today, economics is unequivocally at the core of the forum. In 2009, WEF participants sat together to discuss the elements that triggered the global financial crisis. They agreed on actions that would rectify the situation and avoid further crises.

*"Our role is not to take decisions. We are a platform; we bring together all stakeholders of global society."*
*—Klaus Martin Schwab*

| | |
|---|---|
| Past accomplishments | 7.5/10 |
| International reach | 9/10 |
| Tangibility | 4/10 |
| Peace and hope | 8/10 |
| Building a better world | 7.5/10 |
| Average score | 7.2/10 |

About 90 percent of world trade is conducted on waterways, which offer one of the world's most economic, clean, and safe forms of transport. The International Maritime Organization (IMO) is a UN agency formerly known as the Inter-Governmental Maritime Consultative Organization (IMCO). It is responsible for maritime issues including safety, environmental concerns, legal issues, technical matters, maritime security, and shipping efficiency.

The UN has charged the organization with control of all legal issues regarding their member states and maritime matters. The IMO has 168 member states and three associate members which gather in special committees and sub-committees to evaluate current regulations and adopt new ones. They consult with maritime experts from member states as well as from non-governmental organizations about marine pollution, ship design, training for sailors, and operation standards.

The annual operating budget for the IMO is roughly $87.5 million, less than the cost of a medium-sized oil tanker. Member states contribute to the budget by a percentage that represent's each member's fleet size. Currently, Panama and Liberia have the largest fleets in the world; therefore, their contributions are the greatest.

Examples of important steps in the evolution of marine regulation are: the International Convention for the Safety of Life at Sea, the first treaty of sea safety in 1960; the International Convention for the Prevention of Pollution from Ships of 1973; and the Global Maritime Distress and Safety System, which was introduced in 1988 and became fully operational in 1999.

Today, the IMO ensures that regulations take into consideration new technologies and that treaties are properly implemented by member states. They do not police the field, but provide training, examinations, and certification according to the International Convention on Standards of Training, Certification and Watchkeeping for Seafarers of 1978.

*"Safe, secure and efficient shipping on clean oceans."*
*—Slogan of the IMO*

| | |
|---|---|
| Past accomplishments | 10/10 |
| International reach | 10/10 |
| Tangibility | 2/10 |
| Peace and hope | 6/10 |
| Building a better world | 8/10 |
| Average score | 7.2/10 |

**Right:** Cargo port. 40,000 ships generate an estimated annual income of over $200 billion in freight for the global economy.

The International Civil Aviation Organization (ICAO) is an agency of the United Nations headquarted in Montreal, Canada. It serves as an international forum for civil aviation issues such as safety, secure and sustainable development, environmental protection, and best practices for the industry.

Civil aviation has grown in tandem with tourism and a global economy. Along with the growth of air travel, however, came a need for regulations. Founded in Chicago in 1944, there are over 180 contracting states within the organization today. ICAO members meet every three years to discuss and implement technical and operational aspects of international civil aviation. All civil air travel must adhere to standards of a technical nature, equipment performance, or personnel. Recommended practices are proposed for member states to adapt to their specific situations.

The ICAO also works with other organizations to implement technical programs for aircraft design, programs for aerodrome certification, and fire fighting and emergency planning procedures. They also work toward the efficient exchange of flight safety information, aviation security, environmental damage and control, and audits. The ICAO prioritizes new environmental measures that make the aviation industry secure, safe, and cleaner.

**Left:** Planes flying in a row, ready to land. New York City has the busiest air space in the world, with its three international airports. The Hartsfield–Jackson Atlanta International Airport is the busiest airport in the world.

*"WHEREAS the future development of international civil aviation can greatly help to create and preserve friendship and understanding among the nations and peoples of the world, yet its abuse can become a threat to the general security; and WHEREAS it is desirable to avoid friction and to promote that co-operation between nations and peoples upon which the peace of the world depends; THEREFORE, the undersigned governments having agreed on certain principles and arrangements in order that international civil aviation may be developed in a safe and orderly manner and that international air transport services may be established on the basis of equality of opportunity and operated soundly and economically; HAVE accordingly concluded this Convention to that end."*
—*Introduction of* the Convention on International Civil Aviation, *signed in Chicago on December 7th, 1944*

| | |
|---|---|
| Past accomplishments | 10/10 |
| International reach | 10/10 |
| Tangibility | 2/10 |
| Peace and hope | 6/10 |
| Building a better world | 8/10 |
| Average score | 7.2/10 |

*Patrick Bonneville: Memorial days or veterans' days celebrated all aroud the world teach us about our history—they teach us the value of the contribution of those who lost their lives for us, and they teach that wars have heavy and longlasting consequences.*

On the last Monday in May, the United States observes Memorial Day, a federal holiday in honor of the American men and women who lost their lives during military duty. Originally a day of memorial for the Union soldiers of the American Civil War, it grew to include the remembering of subsequent wars as well. Likewise, Veterans Day is a federal holiday on November 11, when the Armistice that ended World War I is celebrated and fallen soldiers and civilians are remembered.

For some countries of the British Commonwealth, Remembrance Day is a similar celebration. On November 11, veterans, serving members of the military, and members of the public gather at cenotaph war memorials where they observe two minutes of silence at the eleventh hour of the eleventh day of the eleventh month.

The Australia and New Zealand Army Corps honors military heros with Anzac Day on April 25. Created to remember soldiers who fell at Gallipoli, Turkey, during World War I, today it encompasses all those who have lost their lives or have served in military operations for those countries. Anzac Day is also observed in the Cook Islands, Niue, Samoa, and Tonga.

**Opposite page:** Wearing a red poppy.
**Above:** The red poppy became an icon to military veterans after World War I.

*"In Flanders fields the poppies blow between the crosses, row on row, that mark our place; and in the sky the larks, still bravely singing, fly scarce heard amid the guns below."*
*—From In Flanders Fields, a World War I poem written by Lieutenant Colonel John McCrae*

| | |
|---|---|
| Past accomplishments | 8/10 |
| International reach | 7/10 |
| Tangibility | 6.5/10 |
| Peace and hope | 7/10 |
| Building a better world | 7/10 |
| | |
| Average score | 7.1/10 |

The Natural Resources Defense Council (NRDC) is a non-partisan environmental action group with whose goal is to protect the Earth's flora and fauna. Based in New York City, its more than 1.2 million members, 300 lawyers, policy analysts, and scientists work to ensure the Earth's natural resources are used responsibly and sustainably. NRDC uses science and its members' online activism to lobby lawmakers to address critical environmental issues such as global warming, toxic chemicals, ocean health, and awareness of the impact of one's personal environment.

**Above:** NRDC publishes a wide range of publications, including the *Testing The Waters* report. **Right:** Philippe Cousteau Jr., at a NRDC press conference in Santa Monica, California.

Founded in 1970 by law students and attorneys, the NRDC participated in the drafting of early American environment laws. It was named by Worth Magazine as one of America's 100 best charities, and the Wise Giving Alliance of the Better Business Bureau reports that NRDC meets its highest standards for accountability and use of donor funds.

Some current priorities at NRDC include: working to curb global warming by bringing about Amercian legislation that will prohibit environment-damaging industry practices and studying clean energy alternatives; saving wildlands through projects such as Bio-Gems, a citizens' letter-writing program to pressure governments to protect precious ecosystems; working to protect the oceans and to revitalize the damage already done; lobbying for laws that forbid the use of toxic chemicals that

harm the human body and ecosystems; "speeding the greening of China," an initiative to work with that country to reduce its industrial pollution output; and the Green Squad, an educational program in which children learn how to improve the environmental impact made by their schools.

The NRDC's mandate is supported by such public figures as Robert Redford, Leonardo DiCaprio, and GAP director, Robert J. Fisher.

| | |
|---|---|
| Past accomplishments | 7/10 |
| International reach | 6/10 |
| Tangibility | 4/10 |
| Peace and hope | 9/10 |
| Building a better world | 9.5/10 |
| Average score | 7.1/10 |

ionale
tspiele

"NRDC is willing to take on major corporations and the government itself to hold them accountable for the environmental policy that's out there."
—Actor Leonardo DiCaprio

**Left:** The Ceremonial South Pole. The flags of the original signatory nations to the Antarctic Treaty surround it.
**Right:** Taking pictures of Antarctica's natural residents.

*Patrick Bonneville: The Antarctic is of the most remote and unwelcoming places on earth for humanity, yet it is rich for other species. The world is sticking together to protect the white land.*

An essentially hostile environment for humans, Antarctica's lack of resources and isolation have protected it from being permanently claimed by any one state. This continent is considered politically neutral according to the 1959 Antarctic Treaty and other related agreements, collectively called the Antarctic Treaty System (ATS).

As Antarctica has no native population to ensure its well-being, the purpose of the ATS is to protect the lands and promote scientific cooperation between all nations. Today, forty-six countries are part of the treaty, some of which have outposts on the continent or conduct Antarctic research; others have lands that border it in relative proximity. Among other things, the treaty decrees that no nuclear testing or radioactive dumping may take place, and that all scientific research must be done for peaceable ends.

The treaty has also developed guidelines for tourism on the continent: Antarctica is considered an exotic destination, and tourism companies began operating fly-by and ship excursions as early as the 1950's. In recent summer seasons, as many as 46,000 people have visited the land, most of them at the Antarctic Peninsula region from South American ports. This kind of pedestrian traffic can have an negative impact on fragile or limited ecosystems. Guidelines for tourists were established in the early 1990s and are updated regularly.

*"The Parties commit themselves to the comprehensive protection of the Antarctic environment and dependent and associated ecosystems and hereby designate Antarctica as a natural reserve, devoted to peace and science."*
*—Article 2 of the Protocol on Environmental Protection to the Antarctic Treaty (1991)*

| | |
|---|---|
| Past accomplishments | 8/10 |
| International reach | 7.5/10 |
| Tangibility | 4/10 |
| Peace and hope | 7/10 |
| Building a better world | 9/10 |
| | |
| Average score | 7.1/10 |

*"The land looks like a fairytale."*
*—Roald Amundsen (1872—1928)*
*about Antarctica*

Two of the world's great twentieth century enemies united their efforts in 1980 when International Physicians for the Prevention of Nuclear War (IPPNW) was founded. Dedicated to eliminating the nuclear threat to humans, Russian and American cardiologists Dr. Bernard Lown of the Harvard School of Public Health and Dr. Evgueni Chazov of the USSR Cardiological Institute issued a research-based warning to the medical community about the medical impact of nuclear war.

Today, IPPNW is a collective made up of sixty-two national medical organizations who are committed to preventing nuclear war; these organizations represent doctors, medical students, and other health workers who embrace their credo that what the physician cannot heal, he or she must prevent. To this end, IPPNW educates policy makers and the public about the devasting effects of nuclear weapons. With its entry into anti-landmine advocacy in the 1990s, the organization began to extend its mandate to include lobbying and eductating about other kinds of armed violence.

IPPNW was honored with the 1985 Nobel Peace Prize in recognition of their accomplishments.

*"The potential for human devastation from even a single nuclear explosion -- witnessed in the terrible experience of the people of Hiroshima and Nagasaki -- is as real today as it was 60 years ago."*
*—IPPNW*

*"It is the committee's opinion that this organization has performed a considerable service to mankind by spreading authoritative information and by creating an awareness of the catastrophic consequences of atomic warfare."*
*—The Nobel Committee, October 11th, 1985, awarding the Nobel Peace Prize to IPPNW*

**Above:** Protester in protective clothing.
**Opposite page:** Missiles ready to be launched.

| | |
|---|---|
| Past accomplishments | 7.5/10 |
| International reach | 8/10 |
| Tangibility | 4/10 |
| Peace and hope | 7.5/10 |
| Building a better world | 8.5/10 |
| Average score | 7.1/10 |

The Women's International League for Peace and Freedom (WILPF) was founded in 1915 after the Congress of Women was held in The Hague, Netherlands. The conference united some 1,300 women from Europe and North America in their desire for peace in the face of World War I. The women issued a list of resolutions, including a call for disarmament, equality for men and women, and equality among nations. They vowed to carry the resolutions to both warring and neutral European states as well as to the United States.

WILPF evolved into a non-profit, non-governmental organization that works to bring peace to the world by studying the causes of war, exploitation, and oppression. Thirty-seven national sections represent its mission in countries around the world. Its headquarters are in Geneva, Switzerland, with an auxiliary office in New York City.

Almost 100 years ago, the members of WILPF supplied Woodrow Wilson with nine of the fourteen points he proposed for the ending of WWI. They went on to call for the formation of the League of Nations and continue to this day to monitor and contribute to the work of the United Nations, its successor. WILPF has supported and lobbied for women's issues in the Middle East since 1920 and supported the first gathering of indigeonous peoples at the United Nations.

Today, WILPF activism is concentrated in the areas of peace, disarmament, economic justice, environment, racial justice, and human rights. Its members work to ensure that the voices of women are heard with regard to these matters at worldwide summits and in lobbying governments for change. Their aim is "total and universal disarmament," which, their mandate affirms, is the only level of commitment from governments that can lead to real resolutions for other economic and societal problems around the world.

The WILPF has twice received the Nobel Peace Prize for its efforts in working toward a war-free world. The first was awarded to Jane Addams in 1931 and the second to Emily Greene Balch in 1946.

**Above:** Early campaign against nuclear submarine-launched ballistic missiles.
**Upper right:** Ray Acheson, director of *Reaching Critical Will*, the WILPF's program for the abolition of nuclear weapons
**Opposite page:** Woman hoping for peace.

| Past accomplishments | 7/10 |
| International reach | 6.5/10 |
| Tangibility | 5.5/10 |
| Peace and hope | 8.5/10 |
| Building a better world | 7.5/10 |
| | |
| Average score | 7.0/10 |

The International Institute for Sustainable Development (IISD) undertakes research and education in several important areas of sustainable development. It was founded in 1990 in Canada with funding from the Canadian International Development Agency and the province of Manitoba.

The IISD studies changing climate patterns as well as energy consumption and needs. Its goal is to see the creation of sustainable energy sources that do not negatively affect the health of the planet and its atmosphere. It calls for immediate action from all continents in order to eradicate greenhouse gases and develop clean energy. The IISD also studies the economic connections that help organizations and nations to extend their efforts at sustainable development.

Other areas of anaylsis are in foreign investment for sustainable development, the development and sharing of information systems, international trade, natural resources, sustainable markets and trade, natural resources, effects on the environment of political instability, and leadership development in sustainability.

*"Sustainable development is an issue that is crying out for political leadership. We have developed enough experience over the past 20 years to know what to do about most aspects of the issue. We think that the costs are affordable. We have ideas for reform of the system of international environmental governance.Yet history tells us that these ideas do not move without U.S. leadership."*
*—David Runnalls, President & Chief Executive Officer of IISD*

**Upper left:** Young boy standing in a field of wheat looking at windmills in the distance
**Above:** Testing new solar panels.
**Right:** Enjoying the wind and the clean energy.

| | |
|---|---|
| Past accomplishments | 6.5/10 |
| International reach | 7/10 |
| Tangibility | 4/10 |
| Peace and hope | 8.5/10 |
| Building a better world | 9/10 |
| Average score | 7.0/10 |

*Patrick Bonneville: In just a few years, rock star Bono and his friends have become the locomotive of the fight against poverty. They and we have become ONE.*

In 2002, rock singer activist Bono and his friends Bob Geldof, Bobby Shriver, Jamie Drummond, and Lucy Matthew created DATA, standing for "debt, AIDS, trade, Africa." As the name suggests, their mission was to fight for debt relief for poor countries in Africa and to improve trade exchange policies between developed countries and the African continent. They also advocated for issues around AIDS in Africa.

The group took its initiative one step further in 2004. In collaboration with ten other organizations, most of them included in this book, it launched the ONE campaign in the United States. It reached out to American leaders, celebrities, policymakers, and to other activists to rally around one message: developed countries need to do more to help Africa break out of a vicious circle of poverty, debt, illness, and violence. The movement quickly became global, especially with the 2005 success and support of the Live 8 concerts, a series of fundraising music shows held in the G-8 countries. Within less than a year, ONE recruited over 2 million members, giving a stronger voice to the cause.

ONE became such a strongly recognizable name that the organization DATA merged with it in 2007 to form a single body, keeping ONE as the name of the NGO. That year, it acquired a strong ally in the Bill & Melinda Gates Foundation. The organization continues to be a presence at international meetings, reminding politicians and other international actors to keep their promises. ONE representatives participate at conferences of the G-8, G-20, World Economic Forum, and any other significant events.

*"What I'm hoping is that the social movement that is growing around our issues will be so strong that in the event of somebody like me not being around they won't notice. In the end, social movements carry the day, not rock stars."*
—*Bono, in an interview with* Rolling Stone *magazine*

| | |
|---|---|
| Past accomplishments | 4/10 |
| International reach | 9/10 |
| Tangibility | 8/10 |
| Peace and hope | 8/10 |
| Building a better world | 6/10 |
| Average score | 7.0/10 |

**Left:** Co-founder Bono meets with Deloy (14) in Dar es Salaam, Tanzania. The boy lost both of his parents to HIV/AIDS.

For this specialized agency of the United Nations, the weather is the topic of conversation every day. The World Meteorological Organization (WMO) is the world's authoritative voice on the weather as it examines meteorological systems worldwide. One need only look at recent disasters such as severe flooding in India, drought in Eritrea, Hurricane Katrina in the United States, and the disastrous post-earthquake rainy season in Haiti to see how human lives are at the mercy of passing weather events. The WMO analyzes and provides information in the hopes of preventing disasters from such weather-related events.

Established in 1950, the WMO's mandate remains the study of meteorology and the safety and welfare of humanity under weather-related threats. Along with its telecommunications headquarters in Offenbach, Germany, the organization also has eight regional specialized meteorological centers that study and report on weather systems worldwide every day of the year.

**Above:** Weather station (1904m) after a winter storm (Ceahlau, Romanian Carpathians).

The WMO has programs in place to safeguard the environment against natural disasters. It is not usually possible to prevent the damage these events can wreak, but the WMO facilitates cooperation between other organizations to mobilize teams to provide food, safe water, and transport.

WMO encourages the unrestricted exhange of data and information, products and services on matters related to the safety and economic welfare of peoples, as well as the protection of the environment. Its advance warnings have helped save lives and reduced damage to the environment. It also works to reduce the impact of human-induced disasters. Although not weather related, such events as the Exxon Valdez oil disaster, or the Chernobyl nuclear plant explosion do affect our environment and our lives. By combining data, historical research, and current weather patterns, the WMO can inform affected areas about climate trends and weather patterns that can help a region to prepare. A growing facet of WPO's mission is to provide support for developing international programs related to climate change, sustainable development, and other environmental issues.

| | |
|---|---|
| Past accomplishments | 8/10 |
| International reach | 10/10 |
| Tangibility | 5/10 |
| Peace and hope | 3/10 |
| Building a better world | 9/10 |
| Average score | 7.0/10 |

*"Never doubt that a small group of thoughtful, committed citizens can change the world. Indeed, it is the only thing that ever has."*
—Margaret Mead

*Patrick Bonneville: Greenpeace gets the job done. Its members are not afraid to take big risks to get their messages heard.*

A very active and media-prominent organization, Greenpeace seeks to change attitudes and behaviors towards the environment. Probably most known for its goal to protect the world's oceans through the promotion of intelligent fishing and the creation of marine reserves, Greenpeace also advocates the reduction of humanity's dependence on the Earth's resources. It encourages sustainable agriculture, ecologically responsible farming, the elimination of all nuclear weapons, the protection of ancient forests, as well as the protection of the animals and peoples dependent on these forests. It is unapologetically defiant in its drive to create important energy changes that will protect our planet against accelerated climate change.

Greenpeace was created in 1971 as the offspring of a Canadian organization called the "Don't Make a Wave Committee", which was concerned with nuclear testing off the coast of Alaska in 1969. Soon after, Don't Make a Wave joined forces with the Sierra Club, and since the goals of Greenpeace were evolving, the organizations agreed to separate to cover different controversial issues. Today, Greenpeace headquarters are in Amsterdam, the Netherlands, with branch offices in over forty other countries.

**Left:** The Arctic Sunrise at the Copenhagen Summit.

Greenpeace relies on about 2.7 million financial supporters and volunteers to peacefully raise money, campaign governments, hold demonstrations, and do door-to-door soliciting. The organization's administration publicly exposes threats to our environment and researches possible solutions. Greenpeace does not accept funding from governments, corporations, or political parties; rather, funding comes from the donations of individual supporters. In this way, Greenpeace remains close to its roots as an organization completely independent from any political, environmental, or governmental association. Greenpeace intends to have neither permanent allies nor enemies.

Some of Greenpeace's success stories include: bringing about a ban on toxic waste exports to less developed countries; a moratorium on commercial whaling; a United Nations convention providing for better management of world fisheries; a Southern Ocean whale sanctuary; a fifty-year moratorium on mineral exploitation in Antarctica; bans on the dumping at sea of radioactive and industrial waste; an end to high-sea, large-scale driftnet fishing; and its 1996 ban on all nuclear weapons testing.

| | |
|---|---|
| Past accomplishments | 8/10 |
| International reach | 8/10 |
| Tangibility | 3/10 |
| Peace and hope | 7.5/10 |
| Building a better world | 8/10 |
| Average score | 6.9/10 |

The International Maritime Rescue Federation (IMRF) focuses on the sharing of resources and expertise between all of its civilian and military members, both volunteer and paid, that share the goal of the prevention of loss of life at sea. Our seas and oceans are an indispensible resource for humanity, but they are also dangerous. Reliable data shows that about 140,000 lives are lost yearly in maritime disasters, the equivalent of twenty-eight large passenger cruise liners or four hundred modern passenger airplanes.

The IMRF was established in 1924 and counts today over ninety member organizations from sixty countries. Originally known as the International Lifeboat Federation, its name was changed in 2006 to reflect its reincarnation as a charitable organization. Its headquarters are located in Dorset, England.

**Left:** Approximately 71% of the Earth's surface is covered by ocean.
**Above:** U.S. Coast Guard has nearly 42,000 men and women on active duty.
**Right:** An Australian navy sea king helicopter practising a rescue.

The IMRF works with maritime rescue organizations around the world to prevent loss of life at sea, conduct search and rescue missions, and offer financial, technical, and educational support. It teams up with partner organizations to mobilize rescue missions or recuperate wreckage. Through cooperation with its members, it has developed other key areas of activity, including educating people about the risks and dangers of the world's waterways, marine equipment safety, training ships' crews in accident prevention and response, and implementing safety standards and safe operating procedures.

| | |
|---|---|
| Past accomplishments | 8/10 |
| International reach | 7.5/10 |
| Tangibility | 9/10 |
| Peace and hope | 6/10 |
| Building a better world | 4/10 |
| | |
| Average score | 6.9/10 |

*Patrick Bonneville: Fair trade might be the answer to a balanced world; a world where everyone is treated fairly. I agree that we are not there yet, but we are definitely getting closer. Fair trade business is booming. The problem is that not everyone is ready to play fair yet. If we want to do globalization right, the rules must apply to everyone—to every nation, producer, farmer, and distributor.*

In general, fair trade is a market-based and socially organized movement that advocates fair pricing for products that do not disfavor local producers. The movement also incites conumser awareness about the social impact and environmental standards associated with the production, cultivation, and sale of a wide variety of products from around the world.

Currently operating in some seventy countries, the World Fair Trade Organization (WFTO) facilitates market access for members from developing nations or marginalized population groups. This is done through policies and campaigning as well as through marketing and monitoring. Its members represent about 350 organizations who must prove 100 percent participation in

**Left:** Fair trade products in the United States.

fair trade policies. Even after membership is granted, members and products are monitored for adherence to the WFTO's ten principles of fair trade.

Fair trade obligations include supporting marginalized small producers, practicing management and fiscal transparency, standardizing trading practices outlined by the organization, payment of a fair price, ensuring that no forced labor, child labor, or discriminatory hiring practices are used, providing safe working conditions, and maximizing the use of raw materials so as to reduce environmental impact.

The WFTO's FT100 index lists the organizations that represent about 110 million artisans, farmers, growers, producers, and organizations who generate some $2.2 billion in fair trade commerce.

*"Goods produced under conditions which do not meet a rudimentary standard to decency should be regarded as contraband and not allowed to pollute the channels." of international commerce."*
*—Franklin Delano Roosevelt*

| | |
|---|---|
| Past accomplishments | 9/10 |
| International reach | 8/10 |
| Tangibility | 2/10 |
| Peace and hope | 8.5/10 |
| Building a better world | 7/10 |
| | |
| Average score | 6.9/10 |

# WaterAid

Sixty to seventy percent of the human body consists of water. It is safe to say that water is a vital ingredient for human life. Access to clean water is the backbone for health and for the economy, and its role in ending poverty is central.

About 1.1 billion people lack access to safe drinking water, and an estimated 2.6 billion people lack adequate sanitation. Incredibly, some 3900 children die every day from water-borne diseases. In 2002, water was declared a human right. According to the Millenium Development Goals, by 2015 we must reduce by half the number of people without access to clean, safe water and adequate sanitation. WaterAid is a charity that works to meet this goal by operating programs in the poorest countries of Africa, Asia, and the Pacific regions.

WaterAid was officially established as a charitable trust on July 21, 1981 in London, England. By the mid-1980s, WaterAid had developed projects in Ethiopia, Tanzania, Uganda, Sierra Leone, Ghana, Kenya, Bangladesh, Nepal, India, and The Gambia. These projects were possible partly realized through the dedication of volunteer engineers who helped local communities understand and adopt technologies for their environment. An estimated 350,000 people benefited from their efforts.

In 1991, HRH Prince Charles, the Prince of Wales, became the first president of WaterAid. His appointment brought a renewed energy to the organization as he took a personal interest in the projects. By the turn of the century, more than six million people had been directly helped by joint projects on local levels and advocacy at national and international levels to change policies and practices.

For their efforts, WaterAid was the proud recipient of the Charity Times Awards in 2003. By that time, their programs had improved the lives of 7.5 million people.

| | |
|---|---|
| Past accomplishments | 7/10 |
| International reach | 7/10 |
| Tangibility | 8/10 |
| Peace and hope | 7/10 |
| Building a better world | 5/10 |
| Average score | 6.8/10 |

**Right:** Small farmers water their fields using pumps provided by an international aid agency in Mutoko, Zimbabwe.

The GAVI Alliance, formerly the Global Alliance for Vaccines and Immunization, unites groups working on immunization projects that will help people around the world avoid suffering from preventable diseases. This alliance between the public and private sectors includes such partners as the World Bank, the World Health Organization, UNICEF, the Bill & Melinda Gates Foundation, the vaccine industry, civil organizations, and donor and recipient countries.

The GAVI Alliance's simple mission is to ensure that people in poor countries have access to information and vaccines against preventable life-threatening disease. The World Health Organization estimates that since 2000, 3.4 million people have been saved from death because of proper immunization and that about 192.2 million children have been immunized against hepatitis B since GAVI was established. There are currently sixty-seven developing countries receiving GAVI funds to immunize children against hepatitis B.

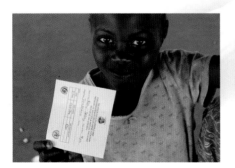

*"If people think you care whether their children live or die, you don't have to send our young people off to war as often."*
*-Bill Clinton*

**Lower left:** Girl proudly showing her vaccination card
**Above:** A health worker vaccinates a toddler against measles in East Nusa Tenggara Province, Indonesia.

*"We now have the evidence that it is possible to rapidly scale up access to vaccines and that even poor countries with few resources can obtain brilliant outcomes if given the opportunity,"*
*—GAVI Executive Secretary Julian Lob-Levyt.*

| | |
|---|---|
| Past accomplishments | 6/10 |
| International reach | 6/10 |
| Tangibility | 8/10 |
| Peace and hope | 7/10 |
| Building a better world | 7/10 |
| Average score | 6.8/10 |

Arms control is the term used to define the management of the production, storage, and use of weapons. Arms control is especially popular for weapons of mass destruction. Arms control should not be confused with disarmament, which is the abolition of weapons.

Signed in 1925, the Geneva Protocol prohibits the use of both chemical and biological weapons, but it falls short of limiting their production, storage or transfer. These items would be addressed much later in the Biological Weapons Convention of 1972 and the Chemical Weapons Convention of 1993.

According to Amnesty International, there are no international arms trade standards that ensure human rights are protected. People the world over fall victim to arms trade—millions through small arms and light weapons, as well as the millions affected by wars.

Amnesty International, Oxfam, and the International Action Network on Small Arms (IANSA) have initiated the Control Arms campaign in the hopes of creating an arms trade treaty specifically calling for strict arms trade and to hold suppliers and dealers accountable. Over 100 countries are for this action and the UN General Assembly has voted in favor of further development.

*"All countries participate in the conventional arms trade and share responsibility for the 'collateral damage' it produces – widespread death, injuries and human rights abuses."*
*—Rebecca Peters, director of the International Action Network on Small Arms (IANSA)*

**Above:** Control Arms campaign poster.
**Upper right:** Event to draw the attention of the G8 leaders meeting in London, 2008.

| | |
|---|---|
| Past accomplishments | 7/10 |
| International reach | 7/10 |
| Tangibility | 4/10 |
| Peace and hope | 8/10 |
| Building a better world | 7/10 |
| Average score | 6.6/10 |

*Patrick Bonneville: Students from all over have shaped the world we live in by campaigning for change. Many student organizations have been created to reflect the visions of young people on important international subjects. This is reassuring, since they are the leaders of tomorrow.*

STAND is the student-led division of the Genocide Intervention Network. It features 850 chapters which are initiated and independently formed within learning institutions in the U.S.A. and in twenty-five other countries. All documents, fund-raising, campaigns, and resources are fully undertaken, solicited, or produced by the students involved. The name STAND stems from the first chapter's mandate: Students Taking Action Now: Darfur, formed at Georgetown University in 2004. In 2006, the name was officially changed to STAND: A Student Anti-Genocide Coalition.

STAND stands firm on the conviction that genocide must be irrevocably eradicated. The only way to achieve this is to hold world leaders responsible for their actions in perpetrating genocide. All of STAND's programs and policies are aligned with the United Nations-endorsed Responsibility to Protect Report, which outlines the responsibility of states to protect their citizens from preventable disasters. When a state refuses or cannot provide this protection, all other nations of the world must act on its behalf.

Chapters introduce students to the mobilization of resources through STAND's Activism 101 program. Here, students learn how to organize, fundraise, advocate, and get media attention. The organization also provides Rapid Responders alerts to members, in which updates on genocide situations and conflict zones around the world are sent electronically to subscribers. STAND also challenges national leaders to take prominent roles in resolving the conflicts that have led to genocide.

*"Your activism challenges the conscience of the world."*
*—Nancy Pelosi*

**Above:** Rally to stop the genocide in Darfur.
**Below:** Campaign stunt sending a message to the American congress.

| | |
|---|---|
| Past accomplishments | 5/10 |
| International reach | 5/10 |
| Tangibility | 6/10 |
| Peace and hope | 10/10 |
| Building a better world | 7/10 |
| | |
| Average score | 6.6/10 |

"This group can speak freely and boldly, working both publicly and behind the scenes on whatever actions need to be taken. Together we will work to support courage where there is fear, foster agreement where there is conflict, and inspire hope where there is despair."
—Nelson Mandela

*Patrick Bonneille: They have been through many world crises. They have improved the world. They have inspired subsequent generations. The voices of wisdom of these honorable women and men can help all of us build a better world for our children.*

The Elders are a group of respected statesmen and women, peace activists, and human rights advocates who offer their collective influence and experience to support peace-building, help address major causes of human suffering, and promote the shared interests of humanity. Members no longer hold public office, which means they are free to speak boldly and with whomever they choose, and to take action that they believe is right. The Elders are committed to listening to ordinary people affected by crisis and conflict, especially women and young people, who so often struggle to be heard. Above all, the Elders inspire others to believe that they can achieve positive change within their own communities.

The idea for The Elders started with entrepreneur Richard Branson and musician Peter Gabriel in 1999 in a conversation about our increasingly interdependent world. They asked themselves whether a small, dedicated group of independent leaders could help the global village to resolve shared problems. For inspiration, they looked to traditional societies, where elders often help to share wisdom and resolve disputes within communities. Gabriel and Branson invited iconic African leader Nelson Mandela and his wife Graça Machel, a women's and children's rights advocate, to bring the Elders together.

The current chair of the twelve-member group is Archbishop Desmond Tutu. The other members are Martti Ahtisaari, Kofi Annan, Ela Bhatt, Lakhdar Brahimi, Gro Brundtland, Fernando H. Cardoso, Jimmy Carter, Graça Machel and Mary Robinson. Nelson Mandela and Aung San Suu Kyi are honorary Elders.

Formally established in 2007, they have focused their peace-building efforts on Burma, Cyprus, the Middle East, Sudan, and Zimbabwe. They have worked to draw attention to the catastrophic risk posed by climate change, especially to future generations, and they are deeply committed to supporting equality between men and women in all aspects of life. They have placed particular emphasis on the responsibility of religious and traditional leaders in changing discriminatory practices.

**Above:** Elders' conference.
**Right:** The Elders in Bil'in. The ground is littered with expired tear gas canisters used by the Israeli military to disperse protesters.

| Past accomplishments | 4/10 |
| --- | --- |
| International reach | 6.5/10 |
| Tangibility | 5.5/10 |
| Peace and hope | 9/10 |
| Building a better world | 8/10 |
| | |
| Average score | 6.5/10 |

*Patrick Bonneville: It is hard for us to see that brutalization and humiliation are acceptable ways toward security and justice. Humanity needs organizations like this in order to persuade governments that torture is not a legitmate means to an end.*

If we look more than two hundred years back into history, we see that most of the world made regular use of torture as a means of punishment and interrogation. While many countries in the West officially abolished the legitimacy of torture in the seventeenth and eighteenth centuries, it is still actively exercised in many countries around the world, especially in developing nations and occasionally even by states who have officially discounted its use.

The Geneva-based World Organisation Against Torture, also known by its French acronym OMCT, was created in 1986. Its mission is to unite NGOs around the world in objecting to the use of torture, executions, kidnapping, and other cruel treatment that impinges upon basic human rights. Its SOS-Torture Network includes nearly 300 organizations on the ground; their many thousands of correspondents report on

| Past accomplishments | 5.5/10 |
|---|---|
| International reach | 6/10 |
| Tangibility | 6/10 |
| Peace and hope | 7.5/10 |
| Building a better world | 7.5/10 |
| Average score | 6.5/10 |

acts of torture that have taken place in their area and propose suitable measures to pressure the governments or entities involved. The OMCT's International Secretariat is alerted to reports of torture every day. It then coordinates appeals through the appropriate financial, political, legal, and media networks that will put pressure on the authorities commiting the torture.

The International Secretariat also offers individual legal assistance to victims of torture and intervenes at the international level with United Nations committees, notably via *amicus curiae*.

OMCT's Urgent Assistance for Victims of Torture program offers individuals medical, social, and legal support. The organization also has an Urgent Campaigns program that focuses on the prevention of torture by working toward compensation for victims and by fighting against the impunity that many authorities using torture take advantage of. OMCT also acts at the diplomatic level through its association with many United Nations committees, the International Labour Organization, the African Commission on Human and Peoples' Rights, the Organisation Internationale de la Francophonie, and the Council of Europe.

**Right:** In 2007, after his retirement from the United Nations, Kofi Annan became the new President of the Foundation supporting the World Organization against Torture (OMCT).

"Intellectual property" is the term given to the legally binding rights held by individuals or collectives for their creative or intellectual work. Rights can be held on works of music, literature, paintings and other fine arts, film, and television, as well as on ideas, discoveries, and inventions. Intellectual property can include copyrights, trademarks, patents and even trade secrets.

The World Intellectual Property Organization (WIPO) is a specialized agency of the United Nations whose purpose is "to encourage creative activity (and) to promote the protection of intellectual property throughout the world." Created in 1967, WIPO currently has 184 member states. The organization replaces the Bureaux Internationaux Réunis pour la Protection de la Propriété Intellectuelle (BIRPI) established in 1893.

The BIRPI itself was formed after foreign exhibitors refused to attend the 1873 International Exhibition of Inventions in Vienna out of fear that their ideas would be stolen and commercially exploited. In 1883, the Paris Convention for the Protection of Industrial Property led to the first international agreement intended specifically for the protection of ideas and creations. It allowed for the protection of patents, trademarks, and industrial designs. Soon after, the Berne Convention for the Protection of Literary and Artistic Works was ratified, ensuring intellectual rights for written works, musical works, and fine art pieces.

WIPO is almost wholly self-financing. It handles international arbitration for IP disputes and analyzes IP legislation and procedures. The organization also provides legal and technical assistance, facilitates the sharing of information about IP throughout the world, and researches technologies that enable the preservation and accessibility of information. Most importantly, perhaps, WIPO works to protect the creators of intellectual properties and ensure the continuation of creation.

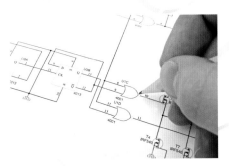

**Above:** according to WIPO, its mission is to promote, through international cooperation the creation, dissemination, use and protection of works of the human mind for the economic, cultural, and social progress of all mankind.

| Past accomplishments | 9/10 |
|---|---|
| International reach | 9.5/10 |
| Tangibility | 2/10 |
| Peace and hope | 5/10 |
| Building a better world | 7/10 |
| Average score | 6.5/10 |

*Patrick Bonneville: Americans produce about 1,676 pounds of garbage per person per year, making the United States the most wasteful nation in the world. Australia, Canada, and most of the European countries follow closely behind.*

The International Solid Waste Association is an independent, non-governmental, non-profit association. Its mission is to contribute to the sustainability of the Earth's environment by promoting and developing effective waste management around the world. From its headquarters in Vienna, Austria, it facilitates the exchange of information on all aspects of waste management between its more than 1,200 members from over ninety countries. Members participate in conferences, meetings, and training programs, where they receive or exchange technical support, research developments, and training.

*"Water and air, the two essential fluids on which all life depends, have become global garbage cans."*
*—Jacques-Yves Cousteau*

Member nations agree to minimize harm to the environment by studying and reporting on the biological treatment of waste material, waste transportation and storage, hazardous waste issues, healthcare waste, legal issues regarding waste management, recycling, thermal treatments, and landfills. The ISWA's Development Program is designed to support developing nations in sustainable waste management through the transfer of knowledge. The ISWA also produces several publications and journals that focus on current waste management issues.

**Upper left:** With increasing population growth and heavy exploitation of natural resources, the need for waste disposal sites is skyrocking.
**Above:** Landfills can pollute the local environment, contaminating groundwater and aquifers.

| | |
|---|---|
| Past accomplishments | 8/10 |
| International reach | 6/10 |
| Tangibility | 4/10 |
| Peace and hope | 7/10 |
| Building a better world | 7.5/10 |
| Average score | 6.5/10 |

Millions of people live as slaves worldwide. It is estimated that at least twelve million are forced into labor, and more than six million of those are children. In its modern form, slavery is most often referred to as human trafficking. It affects most countries of the world, where people are forced into labor as illegal immigrants in sweatshops, prostitution rings, arranged marriages, and, sometimes, illegal international adoption.

Anti-Slavery International (ASI) was founded in 1839 in the United Kingdom. Today, it is a non-governmental organization, charity, and lobby group. Its work focuses exclusively on anti-slavery and related abuse issues. The organization lobbies governments and international agencies to act against slavery and the businesses that profit from human trafficking. It is dedicated to informing and educating the public and its goal is a world without slavery of any kind.

Slavery has been a shameful part of humanity from its earliest known time. Evidence of it can be found in ancient Egypt, Asia, Europe, and Africa, right up to the New World trade of African slaves as late as the nineteenth century. Despite the 1948 Universal Declaration of Human Rights and the 1956 UN "Supplementary Covention on the Abolition of Slavery, the Slave Trade, and Institutions and Practices Similar to Slavery," human trafficking is rampant.

**Left:** Anti-Slavery International is the world's oldest international human rights organization.

Often, the practice is debt-related. A parent, for example, may become indebted in order to pay for the medical care of a sick child or for the facilitation of immigration papers. To repay the debt, the person is forced into labor, for pay which will virtually never amount to the repayment. The debt is then passed down to the next generation. In another example, women or young girls are forced into a marriage where they live a life of servitude. Often, any objection leads to physical or psychological abuse.

Currently, Anti-Slavery International is working on a campaign in Uzbekistan, where the state appears to be endorsing child labor in the cotton-picking industry. As the world's third largest cotton exporter, the nation's schools shut down during the harvest season so that about 200,000 children, some as young as ten years old, can work in the fields. The children who work the hardest might pick enough cotton to earn about fourteen cents a day; those who object are often subjected to beatings. ASI reports that in spite of the country's agreement to ban child labor, it still enjoys the roughly $1 billion profits generated, in part, from forcing children to work in the fields.

| | |
|---|---|
| Past accomplishments | 7/10 |
| International reach | 6/10 |
| Tangibility | 4.5/10 |
| Peace and hope | 7/10 |
| Building a better world | 8/10 |
| Average score | 6.5/10 |

*Patrick Bonneville: On one side, we have the super powers of the G-20. On the other, a group of seventy-seven nations wanting to serve as a counterbalance. It is important that these developing countries group together to defend their interests.*

The Group of 77 evolved from a coalition of seventy-seven countries founded during the United Nations Conference on Trade and Development in June 1964. It is a joint partnership that was created to provide a stronger voice for the smaller nations within the larger context of the UN. The G-77 allows these states to collectively discuss and promote their economic and development interests.

The original group of seventy-seven countries has grown to 130 countries today, from Africa, Asia, Latin America, and the Caribbean. A sub-chapter, the Intergovernmental Group of Twenty-Four on International Monetary Affairs and Development, or G-24, was started in 1971 to deal with issues specific to a group of countries that face difficult financial situations. Although it is not a branch of the International Monetary Fund, the IMF provides some services for the group. While only twenty-four countries are allowed to be members of that group, any member of the G-77 can join its discussions.

The operational structure of the G-77 resembles that of other UN agencies in terms of decision-making, leadership, and membership. The chairmanship

**Above:** Delegates of 77 developing countries held a series of private meetings headed by Mr. Amjad Ali (Pakistan), who was elected first President of the group in 1964.

rotates to a different country each year, and includes members from Africa, Asia, Latin America, and the Caribbean. The group meets annually at the UN headquarters in New York City, and the South Summit, the supreme decision-making body of the group, meets once every five years. The Group of 77 can call special meetings to deal with emergency situations relating to energy, food and agriculture, trade, investments and finance, and science and technology. About once every two years, follow-up conventions are scheduled to analyze progress and to implement new measures arising from discussions.

| | |
|---|---|
| Past accomplishments | 5/10 |
| International reach | 8/10 |
| Tangibility | 4/10 |
| Peace and hope | 8.5/10 |
| Building a better world | 6.5/10 |
| Average score | 6.4/10 |

*Patrick Bonneville: Compassion can change the world. Edmond Kaiser understood this.*

Terre des Hommes, or "Land of Men," is an important international children's relief organization based in Switzerland. The European NGO has divisions in France, Holland, Denmark, Germany, Italy, Luxembourg, Spain, Canada, and Syria. Terre des Hommes has close to 200 employees working in the name of children's rights on 933 projects in sixty-five countries. These projects have been developed in collaboration with 734 local partners.

The organization was created in Lausanne, Switzerland, in 1960. World War II French resistance fighter Edmond Kaiser was devastated in 1959 to learn to story of the children in Algeria. He decided to dedicate his life to less-fortunate children and then created Terre des Hommes, named after the book by Antoine de Saint-Exupéry known in English as *Wind, Sand and Stars*. His organization was created with the vision to help children who were not being helped by existing relief agencies. Kaiser passed away in 2000 at the age of eighty-six.

Today, Terre des Hommes initiates projects that are designed to improve the living conditions of disadvantaged children in their own environments. The organization helps about 300,000 children each year. Terre des Hommes has the ear of the United Nations, UNICEF, the International Labour Organization (ILO), and the Council of Europe.

50 Jahre Einsatz, weiterkämpfen! ▪ 50 ans de lutte, continuons! ▪ 50 anni di lotta, e l'impegno continua! ▪ 50 years' commitment, let's carry on!

**Above:** *T*erres des Hommes report cover.

*"Sitting in the middle of dead or suffering Biafran children, out with the children of Vietnam whose skin has been peeled away by napalm, it would be as if I found it normal to be honored for their martyrdom."*
—*Edmond Kaiser, refusing the French title of Chevalier of the Legion of Honor in 1990*

| | |
|---|---|
| Past accomplishments | 6/10 |
| International reach | 6.5/10 |
| Tangibility | 8.5/10 |
| Peace and hope | 6/10 |
| Building a better world | 5/10 |
| | |
| Average score | 6.4/10 |

*Patrick Bonneville: Thanks to democratic movements, people around the world have succeeded in overthrowing tyrannical governments without significant violence. By protesting and by taking to the streets, people have succeeded in taking their countries and their lives into their own hands.*

*One important man who showed the way of non-violent resistance is the "Father of India," Mohandas Karamchand Gandhi—Mahatma Gandhi. He led a non-violent political movement in India to end British colonial rule. His approach was that of* Satyagraha, *which means "demand for truth." Millions followed him in boycotting anything British—commercial goods, schools, courts, taxes. Gandhi led this non-violent campaign until the independence of India in 1947. He was assassinated just a few days later, on January 30, 1948, by Nathuram Godse, a Hindu radical empassioned by the political partitioning of Pakistan from India.*

Mahatma Gandhi was born in British India on October 2, 1869. Today, his birthday is celebrated as a national holiday in India and as the International Day of Non-Violence around the world. The United Nations General Assembly named October 2 the International Day of Non-Violence in 2007 to honor Ghandi's legacy of peace. All members of the UN are encouraged to celebrate "in an appropriate manner... the message of non-violence, including through education and public awareness."

In September 2009, in anticipation of the International Day of Non-violence, the Secretary-General of the United Nations Ban Ki-Moon issued a revolutionary appeal to non-violence. He referred to the greenhouse gas emissions issued by our manufacturing and energy industries as part of the "human assault on our planet." He urged environmental activists everywhere to appeal to their government leaders to agree to universal measures at the UN Climate Change Conference of that year. He also implied that the public, as well, should embrace non-violence in its use of the earth's resources in the face of "catastrophic climate change."

| | |
|---|---|
| Past accomplishments | 3.5/10 |
| International reach | 9/10 |
| Tangibility | 2.5/10 |
| Peace and hope | 8.5/10 |
| Building a better world | 8.5/10 |
| Average score | 6.4/10 |

Wetlands are often considered the most diverse of all ecosystems. Their plants serve as virtual water purifiers and control flooding; they also provide shelter and food for an important variety of creatures ranging from water dewellers to land animals and air creatures, who, in turn, keep the wetlands fertile. All around the world, governments and organizations work hard to protect our wetlands and promote their necessity for the planet's health.

The Ramsar Convention was conceived specifically for the protection, conservation, and sustainable utilization of the world's wetlands. Named after the town of Ramsar in Iran, the convention draws international attention to the essential value of our wetlands. The convention lists some 1,801 sites around the world that together cover an area of about 1,630,000 square kilometers. The United Kingdom has the largest number of sites, with 166, while Canada has the largest land area of wetlands, with over 130,000 square kilometers in total. The African country Chad comes a close second.

Because wetlands have little commercial value as they are, they are often destroyed and turned into real estate developments or flooded and used as man-made lakes. Wetland conservationists understand and try to promote the importance of these fragile environments in our ecosystems.

**Above:** The effects of de-forestation on wetlands. 50% of the world's wetlands are estimated to have disappeared since 1900.

*"The Convention's mission is the conservation and wise use of all wetlands through local and national actions and international cooperation, as a contribution towards achieving sustainable development throughout the world."*
—*The Ramsar Convention*

| | |
|---|---|
| Past accomplishments | 8/10 |
| International reach | 7/10 |
| Tangibility | 3/10 |
| Peace and hope | 6/10 |
| Building a better world | 8/10 |
| Average score | 6.4/10 |

"*We opened the hatch. Sergei Krikalev was with me. I just waved my hand toward the hatch and the two of us entered together . . . I think what the space station talks about is international cooperation: there wasn't a first person in; we went in together.*"
—*Bob Cabana, Colonel (USMC) Ret., American astronaut and director of NASA's John F. Kennedy Space Center.*

*Kimberly Murray: The drive to explore led humanity from the heart of Africa into the rest of the world. By the twentieth century we had explored our planet's highest peaks and deepest ocean floors. Then, about fifty years ago, the dream of exploring beyond the earth was realised with the onset of space exploration.*

*At an orbit of more than 400 kilometers above the Earth, the space station is visible from most countires. You just have to know where and when to look. For more information, visit http://www. spaceflight.nasa.gov/realdata/sightings/.*

In an inspiring spirit of international cooperation, scientists have begun work on the largest space station ever built. Once fully constructed, the International Space Station will measure 108 by 74 meters and will have 1,250 cubic meters of living and working space—about the size of a Boeing 747. The station is powered by solar panels. Construction began in 1998 and is scheduled for completion around 2015—it will have taken an estimated fifty missions to build the station.

**Above:** International dinner in space.
**Opposite page:** Destination: International Space Station.

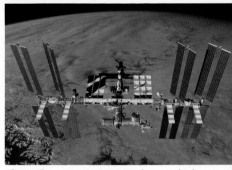

**Above:** The station is maintained at an orbit between 278 km (173 mi) and 460 km (286 mi) altitude

The space station is a prime example of unity and cooperation. Seventeen dedicated space programs from the United States (NASA), Russia (RKA), Japan (JAXA), Canada (CSA), and the eleven European countries of ESA (Belgium, Denmark, France, Germany, Italy, the Netherlands, Norway, Spain, Sweden, Switzerland, and the United Kingdom), Brazil (AEB), and Italy (ASI) all work together to make the project possible.

The purpose of the International Space Station is to serve as a research laboratory. In 1992, then-President George H.W. Bush of the U.S.A. and Russian President Boris Yeltsin agreed that the time had come for a joint agreement between the two nations. Their first project in cooperation saw an American astronaut board the Russian space station MIR, and, later, two Russian cosmonauts board an American space shuttle. One year later, in 1993, the International Space Station was co-presented by the U.S.A. and Russia, although it eventually counted several other countries as well.

| Past accomplishments | 9/10 |
| International reach | 6/10 |
| Tangibility | 2/10 |
| Peace and hope | 8/10 |
| Building a better world | 7/10 |
| | |
| Average score | 6.4/10 |

*Patrick Bonneville: Mother Nature is the mother of all mothers. She gives us nourishment. She gives us drink. She gives us warmth and shelter. She is strong, yet fragile. She needs to be honored every day, but she needs a big celebration at least once a year.*

**Above:** Celebration at Grand Central Station, New York.
**Right:** Girl holding a NASA Earth Ball on Earth Day, Savannah, Georgia.

Earth Day is celebrated in many countries around the world each year. The first Earth Day was celebrated in the United States at the insistence of U.S. Senator Gaylord Nelson of Wisconsin, considered a pioneer in environmental activism. Nelson initiated, in 1969, the notion of "teach-ins" about environmentalism. He proposed the first Earth Day a short time later, on April 22, 1970.

For the first Earth Day, the mayor of New York City agreed to close Fifth Avenue to traffic, to accommodate a rally. More rallies across the country were attended by an estimated twenty million citizens. The day was an astounding success and underlined the true concern the American people held for the environment. The success of this first Earth Day led to a long-lasting belief among various environmental groups that their efforts resonate with the general population.

Twenty years later, on April 22, 1990, more than 200 million people in 141 countries held events to commemorate Earth Day. This event helped increase awareness for the 1992 United Nations Earth Summit in Rio de Janeiro.

While Earth Day has focused on environmental issues since its inception in 2000, a bigger picture was adopted as the campaign grew to focus on global warming and clean energy. With the help of the Internet, some 5,000 environmental groups from around the world joined the cause. A record 184 countries participated, drawing hundreds of millions of demonstrators. By 2007, an estimated one billion people worldwide celebrated Earth Day.

Earth Day Network members include NGOs, government agencies, activists, and people from the general public. The Network works year-round to raise awareness and encourage activism in environment-related issues. Currently, an estimated 19,000 organizations in 192 countries participate in Earth Day Network education and field-work programs.

| Past accomplishments | 5/10 |
| International reach | 8/10 |
| Tangibility | 2/10 |
| Peace and hope | 8/10 |
| Building a better world | 9/10 |
| | |
| Average score | 6.4/10 |

*Patrick Bonneville: The rain forests are one of the Earth's greatest treasures. Let's be unified in helping the countries that host them protect them.*

Rainforests are sometimes referred to as the "jewels of the Earth" and the "world's largest pharmacy." Indeed, a large number of our natural medicines hail from rainforests. An incredible 28 percent of the world's oxygen is processed through rainforests. These natural spaces are essential to our survival—even for those of us who live thousands of miles away.

The Rainforest Coalition is an association of developing nations who have rainforests within their borders and industrialized nations who support fair trade and economic development outside their own borders. Formed in 2005 and with a secretariat in New York City, the Coaltion unites experts from governments, academia, and industry to address rainforest issues at conferences, seminars, and in collaborative programs. They share research and ideas about rainforest management, conservation of biodiversity, climate stability, the alleviation of poverty, and sustainable exploitation of the rainforests' resources.

Their efforts are essential; rainforests are havens for much of life on Earth. Estimates suggest that 40 to 75 percent of all species on the planet are native to rainforests. Scientists estimate that there are millions more species yet to be discovered.

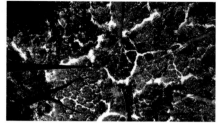

**Above:** Up to 75% of all species on Earth are indigenous to the rainforests.

The Coalition institutes specific measures to ensure that participating countries have equal basis for exploitation. It also advises on the advancement of sustainable development solutions that will help improve the living standards for rainforest communities and develop long-term security for them, and serve as an example for other deforested nations.

Similar to the Rainforest Coalition, the Rainforest Alliance is specifically interested in changing commercial behavior as a means of protecting our rainforests. The Alliance works directly with those people whose lives are interwoven with the land. Through projects based on education and information, the Alliance demonstrates how to change habits and create profitable enterprises while maintaining the integrity of the forests that they so need.

| | |
|---|---|
| Past accomplishments | 6/10 |
| International reach | 6/10 |
| Tangibility | 3/10 |
| Peace and hope | 8/10 |
| Building a better world | 9/10 |
| Average score | 6.4/10 |

*Patrick Bonneville: Tourism is the biggest industry in the world. Money flows with travelers from one country to another. But with tourism comes the great responsibility of respecting the people and the environment of the host country.*

There will be 1.6 billion international tourist arrivals worldwide by 2020. The need to develop international standards and ethics for the tourism industry is obvious, especially when considering the impact this kind of traffic must have on the Earth.

The World Tourism Organization (UNWTO ) is a specialized agency of the United Nations that promotes responsible, sustainable, and universally accessible tourism. It makes special efforts to consider the concerns of developing nations. Based in Madrid, Spain, UNWTO was established on January 2, 1975, to promote tourism as a means to economic development, international understanding, and peace. It currently includes 161 member countries and territories as well as more than 370 affiliate members from the private sector, educational institutions, tourism associations, and authorities.

The UNWTO's major initiatives include the implementation of education programs  designed to further tourism-based education within member states, as well as improve the quality, competitiveness, and sustainability of tourism worldwide. UNWTO also implemented the Global Code of Ethics for Toursim. This guide outlines how member states can benefit from the economic advantages of tourism and derive positive social and cultural effects, as well as the measures that will preserve their natural and cultural heritage.

*Most visited countries based on international tourist arrivals*

| Rank | Country | Intl. arrivals |
|------|---------|----------------|
| 1 | France | 81.9 million |
| 2 | Spain | 59.2 million |
| 3 | U.S.A. | 56.0 million |
| 4 | China | 54.7 million |
| 5 | Italy | 43.7 million |

*Source: UNWTO*

| | |
|---|---|
| Past accomplishments | 7/10 |
| International reach | 10/10 |
| Tangibility | 2/10 |
| Peace and hope | 5/10 |
| Building a better world | 8/10 |
| Average score | 6.4/10 |

**Left:** Europe and the Americas account for over 75% of the global tourism market.

*Kimberly Murray: There are lyrics to a rather famous song that ask us to imagine all people living life in peace. It seems hard to imagine something so grand, so immeasurable ever happening. But all it takes is one first step.*

In 1891, the International Peace Bureau (IPB) was created as a united front that would face international issues with an unbiased mandate. Its efforts have not fallen on deaf ears; the founders of the organization were the 1910 Nobel Peace laureate recipients, and over the course of its history, thirteen IPB officers have been awarded the same honor.

Based in Geneva, IPB is the world's oldest peace organization. It is no stranger to the world's most powerful associations of nations: the IPB fearlessly voiced criticism of the League of Nations and, later, the United Nations, when it felt that corruption or manipulation from big states interfered with advances in peace.

IPB brings together 282 member organizations from seventy countries worldwide. Its current priority is "sustainable disarmament for sustainable develoment." The IPB has consultative status with the UN Economic and Social Council and associate status with the UN's Department of Public Information and with UNESCO. It plays a key role in the Geneva-based NGO Committee for Disarmament and the Conference of NGO in Consultative Status with ECOSOC, and keeps close contacts with sister organizations in New York. IPB also offers member organizations the opportunity to address the UN Commission on Human Rights.

*"It is a great honour to be asked to chair such a long-standing and prestigious organization. The world faces extraordinary new security challenges and the international peace movement must work even harder to develop fresh and effective forms of cooperation."*
*—Tomas Magnusson, President of the International Peace Bureau*

**Above:** 2010 was the 100th anniversary of the 1910 Nobel Peace Prize, awarded to the International Peace Bureau.

| | |
|---|---|
| Past accomplishments | 7/10 |
| International reach | 7/10 |
| Tangibility | 3/10 |
| Peace and hope | 7/10 |
| Building a better world | 8/10 |
| Average score | 6.4/10 |

**Left:** All over the world, infants and toddlers drown more frequently than any other age group. The vast majority of drownings occur in open water– the sea, lakes, ponds, rivers. A red flag on the beach means rough conditions .

Humans use water as a means of transport, energy, and for agriculture, as well as for the hydration of our bodies and for pleasure. But humans are not born natural swimmers; we need to learn to swim and to survive in the water. The International Life Saving Federation (ILS) was created to be a world authority on water safety and lifesaving expertise.

The ILS was born from the 1994 merger of two other long-lived organizations: the Fédération Internationale de Sauvetage Aquatique (FIS), formed in 1910, and World Life Saving (WLS), formed in 1971. Now, the ILS cooperates with partner organizations, governments, non-government organizations, and sponsors to promote water safety around the world.

It also works to standardize safety laws, symbols used for signage, and equipment and information regarding water safety. It participates in international congresses and competitions with the intention of creating a community between members and their humanitarian partners. The ILS also supports environmental measures to clean our beaches and waterways of pollution and related dangers to the public.

Training is an important aspect of the work of the ILS: it saves lives by organizing training for emergency lifesaving techniques and drowning and water accident prevention. According to the ILS, over 1,000,000 rescues are made each year by lifeguards certified by the federation's training programs.

*"Where the earth meets the sea, where the waves meet the sky, where people meet the water, we'll be standing by. Wherever life's in need, wherever waters flow, our circle will hold fast and true, with strength we'll grow."*
*—Excerpt of "Stand Inside the Circle", the ILS's official song*

| | |
|---|---|
| Past accomplishments | 6.5/10 |
| International reach | 7/10 |
| Tangibility | 8.5/10 |
| Peace and hope | 4/10 |
| Building a better world | 6/10 |
| | |
| Average score | 6.4/10 |

The International Monetary Fund (IMF) is a private, member-based organization that monitors global financial systems. This international organization was formed to help stabilize exchange rates, facilitate the development of economic policies, and offer financial and technical aid to it members, which it does by offering economic surveillance, technical assistance and training, and money lending.

Founded in 1944 in Washington, DC, the fund was created in response to the Great Depression of the 1930s, when international trade was weakened because countries were hesitatant to participate in foreign trade. Trade barriers rose and the standard of living in many countries suffered. To prevent further such economic disaster from occurring again, the fund was set up. As a consequence, stability grew in global trade markets and the fund itself grew greatly as well, with the joining of newly independent African nations in the 1950s and 60s.

After the fall of the Berlin wall in 1989 and the dissolution of the Soviet Union, membership in the IMF was nearly global. Today, IMF membership stands at 185 countries, just a few short of universal membership. This provides great flexibility and opportunities; they are well-placed as a forum for the exchange of ideas, support, and action and to keep members appraised of potential problems.

The IMF works in partnership with other international organizations, including the World Bank, the World Trade Organization, UN agencies, and regional development banks. Where the World Bank is concerned with long-term development and reducing poverty, however, the IMF is focused on macroeconomics and financial sector issues.

*"The day is not far off when the economic problem will take the back seat where it belongs, and the arena of the heart and the head will be occupied or reoccupied, by our real problems - the problems of life and of human relations, of creation and behavior and religion."*
*—British economist John Maynard Keynes (1883 – 1946), one of the founding fahers of the IMF and the World Bank.*

| | |
|---|---|
| Past accomplishments | 7/10 |
| International reach | 7/10 |
| Tangibility | 3/10 |
| Peace and hope | 7/10 |
| Building a better world | 8/10 |
| Average score | 6.4/10 |

**Right:** Members of 45 governments met at the Mount Washington Hotel in July 1944 to create IMF.

*Patrick Bonneville: This organization and its people believe that we need to protect our land and water.*

Based in the United States, this environmental organization was founded in 1951 with one simple but very important goal: to protect and preserve land and water so that the diversity of life that supports our planet will prevail. The Nature Conservancy has 720 staff scientists and works in thirty-two countries. With over one million members, it has a reputation as one of the best-managed charities in the United States.

So far, the Nature Conservancy has protected more than 119 million acres of land and 5,000 miles of rivers all over the world. The group is active in each of the United States; in Canada, it focuses on Boreal forests, including the unique Great Bear Rainforest in British Columbia. It has saved land in Mexico and Central and South America. The Nature Conservancy helped to establish the Morne Trois Piton National Park in Dominica in 1974 and works in the Caribbean, where countries have committed to protecting nearly 20 percent of their marine and coastal habitat.

| | |
|---|---|
| Past accomplishments | 6/10 |
| International reach | 5/10 |
| Tangibility | 5/10 |
| Peace and hope | 7/10 |
| Building a better world | 8.5/10 |
| Average score | 6.3/10 |

**Right:** Nature Conservancy campaign.

In Africa, the Nature Conservancy offers a variety of programs, including "Adopt an Acre in East Africa." In collaboration with its partners, the African Wildlife Foundation, the Lewa Conservancy, and the Northern Rangelands Trust, the Nature Conservancy buys land in order to protect wild areas in East Africa's Rift Valley. This rainforest region is home to some of the greatest biodiversity in the world.

The Nature Conservancy is also present in Asia, where it works in China, Mongolia, Australia, Indonesia, Micronesia, Papua New Guinea, and in the Solomon Islands. The group works on land and under the sea, making sure our most valuable natural treasures are protected in every corner of the world.

LET'S SAVE THE PLANET
ONE ACRE AT A TIME

What if everyone took responsibility for one small piece of the planet?

Now, you can do your part. When you Adopt an Acre," you help the The Nature Conservancy preserve the diversity of life on Earth, in places close to home, and around the world.

To adopt your acre, visit nature.org/adopt

The Nature Conservancy
Protecting nature. Preserving life.

## Medicines for Malaria Venture

Established in 1999 in Switzerland, the Medicines for Malaria Venture (MMV) is a non-profit foundation dedicated to reducing malaria in disease-endemic countries. It is a public-private partnership that brings together the pharmaceutical industry with public resources to research, develop, and facilitate the discovery and distribution of effective antimalarial drugs. Its partnerships include governments, private foundations, international organizations, and corporate foundations.

Forty percent of the world's population lives in countries where malaria is present, and it is estimated that the disease kills a child every thirty seconds. Six hundred million new infections are recorded worldwide annually. Ninety percent of malaria-related deaths are in Sub-Saharan Africa, with the disease growing in Asia and Latin America.

Malaria is transmitted to humans by female anopheles mosquitoes infected with malaria parasites; they are the only kind of mosquito to transmit the disease. Symptoms include fever, chills, headache, muscle aches, fatigue and sometimes nausea, vomiting and diarrhea. Malaria can also lead to anemia and jaundice. Without immediate treatment, the strain Plasmodium falciparum can lead to coma or even death.

Malaria has always been a health threat to humanity. There are records of the disease in China a far back as 5,000 years ago. The search for treatment is also long. First used in the seventeenth century, quinine was the main treatment for malaria up to 1940. Because of its unpredictable effects, scientists began to look for an alternative. After World War II, chloroquine and DDT were introduced as medicines that would eradicate malaria around the world, and the WHO began spraying DDT in malaria zones. In the early 1970s, when DDT was revealed to be linked to certain cancers, the chemical was banned by the WHO. DDT is nevertheless still used today in certain parts of the world as a means for mosquito control.

Other drugs have been developed but the malaria parasites have been shown to develop a resistance to them. Artemisnin is used today in most Asian countries to combat malaria. MMV is active in the creation of synthetic drugs that will likely be the next level of attack against malaria. These treatments show promise in eradicating the disease; they are safer, more efficient, and less expensive than the traditional drugs currently available.

| | |
|---|---|
| Past accomplishments | 5/10 |
| International reach | 7.5/10 |
| Tangibility | 7.5/10 |
| Peace and hope | 5/10 |
| Building a better world | 6.5/10 |
| | |
| Average score | 6.3/10 |

Although many agencies calling themselves "humane societies" exist around the world, the most well known in North America is the organization dedicated to the prevention of cruelty to animals. In many countries, such as Canada, the United States, the United Kingdom, Australia, and New Zealand, the Humane Society is officially known as the Society for the Prevention of Cruelty to Animals (SPCA).

The Humane Society International is the international branch of the Humane Society of the United States. It operates offices in many countries worldwide and is the world's largest organization dedicated to the protection of animals. They have the support of over 10.5 million people and consider themselves the human voice for animals. Through education, investigation, advocacy, and hands-on work, Humane Societies actively seek improved living conditions for wild, domestic, and marine animals the world over.

The first Humane Society in the United States was founded in New York in 1866. Canada's first SPCA was founded in Montreal in 1869. In Australia, it was founded in 1871. Early British settlers in New Zealand included animal protection

**Lower left:** Humane Society response after the 2010 Haiti Earthquake.
**Above:** Rescue operations after the passage of Huricanne Katrina.
**Below:** Puppy awaiting adoption.

in their laws of 1835, and in the United Kingdom, protection acts were signed as far back as the eighteenth century. The United Kingdom's Royal Humane Society was founded in 1774, and the Royal Society for the Prevention of Cruelty to Animals followed in 1824.

Each organization operates under its own mandate and mission statement. Generally speaking, humane societies provide refuge for sick and abandoned animals and go to great lengths to heal and find suitable homes for them. They are usually charitable organizations that rely heavily on private donations.

An often unrecognized area of work by the Humane Society is that of disaster services. Through preparedness programs and animal training, the Humane Society can go into regions struck by disaster and lead rescue efforts for affected animals.

| Past accomplishments | 6/10 |
| International reach | 6.5/10 |
| Tangibility | 7/10 |
| Peace and hope | 4/10 |
| Building a better world | 8/10 |
| | |
| Average score | 6.3/10 |

The sale and trade of wildlife—both flora and fauna—is lucrative and charged with issues: it is often the recourse for impoverished or uneducated peoples with no other source of revenue. As an impartial worldwide organization, TRAFFIC works to restrict the illegal trade of plants and animals that can negatively affect our environment. Its philosophy is that the trade of animals and wild plants is legitimate if it is well managed; to this end, TRAFFIC is guided by the Convention on International Trade in Endangered Specieis of Wild Fauna and Flora (CITES).

We cannot damage, any further, an already fragile ecosystem, nor can we harm the sustainable environments necessary for healthy conservation. Established in 1976, TRAFFIC has grown into a leader in conservation with projects in about thirty countries. They are impartial and action-oriented: research is done in the field and applied to projects in the field. The organization's governing committee includes representation from partner organizations, WWF and IUCN, who set priorities relating to wildlife trade issues.

The trade of animals, including live species, and plants and other organisms generates billions of dollars in revenue. They are often used in products, such as medicine, or as tourist souvenirs, timber, food, or other such items. According to the United Nations Food and Agriculture Organization, timber and seafood are the most traded.

**Left:** Animal fur for sale in a South African shop.

Illegal trade activity is typically concentrated along China's international borders, East and Southern Africa, Southeast Asia, parts of the eastern borders of the European Union, and some areas of Mexico, the Caribbean, Indonesia, New Guinea, and the Solomon Islands. While TRAFFIC imposes appropriate penalties when infractions are discovered, they also work to encourage local governments and organizations to develop sustainable projects other than illegal trade.

*"As human populations have grown, so has the demand for wildlife. People in developed countries have become used to a lifestyle which fuels demand for wildlife; they expect to have access to a variety of seafoods, leather goods, timbers, medicinal ingredients, textiles etc. Conversely, extreme poverty of others means they regard wildlife as a means to meet their short-term needs and will trade it for whatever they can get."*
*—TRAFFIC*

| | |
|---|---|
| Past accomplishments | 8/10 |
| International reach | 9/10 |
| Tangibility | 2/10 |
| Peace and hope | 5/10 |
| Building a better world | 7/10 |
| Average score | 6.2/10 |

*Kimberly Murray: Humanity has awakened to the urgency of environmental issues. We have created new terms, such as global footprint, sustainable development, greenhouse effect. These terms reflect the impact we have on the world around us. The need to protect our environment is not only for the present; indeed, it is for the future.*

In 1974, The Worldwatch Institute began researching and documenting the environmental issues that would increasingly endanger the planet. Its findings and recommendations about global security, food issues, population growth, manufacturing and consumption, and the natural environment are transmitted to policy makers, the business community, and NGOs. This has led the organization to be recognized as one of the top ten sustainable development research bodies in the world.

The Worldwatch Institute counsels governments, policy makers, business communities, and organizations on strategies for creating a sustainable society. It observes and reports on issues such as climate change, resource degradation, population growth, and poverty. Some of the organization's projects are oriented toward building a low-carbon energy system and ensuring healthy and sustainable agricultural practices and a sustainable economy. It also monitors human health, population, water resources, biodiversity, governance, and environmental security.

Worldwatch provides the public updates on environmental sustainability news and events through its online news service called *Eye on Earth,* a sister service to *World Watch* magazine. In partnership with Blue Moon Fund, a philanthropic foundation, the magazine offers a unique perspective on events, research, and global trends in the environment. The organization also produces *Global in Focus,* an international publication circulated in 36 languages by 150 partners in 40 different countries. Worldwatch publishes a third periodical entitled *State of the World,* a resource for global policy makers and for citizens concerned about the environment.

**Upper right:** *State of the World* is the Worldwatch's flagship publication

| | |
|---|---|
| Past accomplishments | 8/10 |
| International reach | 8/10 |
| Tangibility | 4/10 |
| Peace and hope | 7/10 |
| Building a better world | 4/10 |
| Average score | 6.2/10 |

*Patrick Bonneville: This organization might not receive as much of the spotlight as other organizations fighting for children's rights, such as UNICEF or Save The Children, but Plan does tremendous work. Millions of children benefit from its programs, making Plan a significant leader in building a better world.*

To millions of children and families in forty-eight developing countries in Africa, Asia, and the Americas, Plan is much more than a name. It is a means to change. Plan is the oldest and largest NGO working for children's rights and has a staff of over 6,000 people worldwide and over 50,000 volunteers. It is based in the United Kingdom, from where it has improved many lives since its foundation in 1937.

This great endeavor began in Spain, during the Spanish Civil War. Two men, John Langdon-Davies, a journalist covering the war, and Eric Muggeridge, a volunteer helping refugees, wanted to do more to help children who were suffering from this war. They created a sponsor-child program to provide food and accommodation to the children of the Spanish Civil War. The sponsoring program continues to this day, with over one million donors from eighteen countries.

Plan aims to assist the less fortunate children of the world in reaching their full potential by helping them to build a better life and breaking the circle of poverty. Besides child sponsorship, Plan has successfully implemented education, health, and protection programs.

The organization works closely with the United Nations and other partners to the Convention on the Rights of the Child. These rights include the right to survive, to develop to the fullest, to be protected from harmful influences, abuse, and exploitation, and to participate fully in family, cultural, and social life.

*"He loved children so much. That is why he mobilised his friends and acquaintances to write letters to the orphaned and underprivileged children while raising money for their education."*
*—Debbie Langdon-Davies, speaking of her father, John Langdon-Davies*

**Above:** Young girls supported by Plan Espana.

| | |
|---|---|
| Past accomplishments | 6/10 |
| International reach | 5/10 |
| Tangibility | 8/10 |
| Peace and hope | 6/10 |
| Building a better world | 6/10 |
| Average score | 6.2/10 |

*Kimberly Murray: This entry is not about one particular group but, rather, a category. We think that collectively, these poltical parties deserve mention as an honorable presence in our world.*

A Green Party is a formally recognized political party whose platform is first and foremost one of environmental advocacy, or "green politics." More than just ecology, however, a Green Party also focuses on grassroots democracy, non-violence, and social justice. Its agenda often gives priority to the rights of indigenous people, as well as to the basic rights of all people and animals, and to ensuring that all citizens have access to systems that ensure their good health and the health of our ecosystems.

The first green-biased party was established in Tasmania in 1972. It was formed in response to the government's proposed flooding of Lake Peddler for a dam project. Although its members were not able to create a political party in time for the upcoming election, or stop the flooding and creation of the dam, they certainly caused a stir in the political status quo, securing 3.9 percent of the vote. Two years later the group was recognized as an official party and in 1983 was successful in stopping another hydroelectric projet.

In May of 1972, the Values Party, the world's first official Green Party, was founded in New Zealand. Although its efforts to win seats in various elections failed, its transformation in 1990 to the Green Party of Aotearoa New Zealand brought success. After winning support—but no seats—in the 1990 election, the party found new hope for its efforts. In 1999, it secured seven seats, which meant it was eligible for more funding.

The Global Green Network (GGN) was established in 2001 in Canberra, Australia, to provide support and communication exchanges among Green Parties around the world. Through the sharing of information and strategies, national parties can better understand how to advance their platform and win support with the public. Today, twenty-four parties are members of the Global Green Network: Benin, Cameroun, Chad, Mauritania, Mauritius, Morrocco, Somalia, Tunisia, Brazil, Canada, Chile, Dominican Republic, Mexico, Peru, United States, Uraguay, Mongolia, New Zealand, New Caledonia, Austria, Finland, Germany, Hungary, Netherlands, Poland, Spain, Sweden, and Switzerland.

| Past accomplishments | 5/10 |
|---|---|
| International reach | 8/10 |
| Tangibility | 3/10 |
| Peace and hope | 7/10 |
| Building a better world | 7.5/10 |
| Average score | 6.1/10 |

## International Organization for Standardization

*Kimberly Murray: Who among us has not seen the ISO signs posted along highways and in industrial parks? Now we know what they mean: they help ensure that companies, industries, and governments are playing a fair game in the marketplace.*

The International Organization for Standardization, or ISO, is an independent entity that analyzes, develops, and publishes international standards on many different things. Standards offer consumers and manufacturers an assurance of uniformity and quality; specific benefits may include fair prices for goods, health and environment improvements, sustainablility practices, and equal trading regulations between nations. Standards might be applied to such things as quality control, environmental sustainability, safety, reliability, efficiency, and interchangeability. Conformity to some standards is voluntary, for others it is not.

*"ISO enables a consensus to be reached on solutions that meet both the requirements of business and the broader needs of society."*
*—The International Organization for Standardization*

As the world's largest standards developing organization, the ISO serves as a bridge between the public and private sectors. It is composed of national standards institutes from 161 countries. Since 1947, it has published over 17,500 international standards for such diverse industries as agriculture, construction, engineering, medical devices, and information technology. ISO promotes standardization in three main areas: products, processes, and management systems.

Once a company has obtained ISO certification, it is bound to its norms. Industries and companies are eager to achieve the stamp of approval that ISO certification endows, as it shows their commitment to quality to the international world of trade.

*"The essence of ISO's history is made up of the visions, aspirations, doubts, successes, and failures of the people who, over the past fifty years, have created this rather remarkable organization."*
*—The late Lawrence D. Eicher, former ISO Secretary-General*

| | |
|---|---|
| Past accomplishments | 7.5/10 |
| International reach | 9/10 |
| Tangibility | 3/10 |
| Peace and hope | 3/10 |
| Building a better world | 8/10 |
| | |
| Average score | 6.1/10 |

Voluntary Service Overseas (VSO) is an international charity whose strategy in the fight against poverty is to place volunteers in communities in developing countries. It is the largest volunteer-partnering organization in the world and was given the 2004 top international development charity award at the UK Charity Awards.

Since its creation in 1958, when England's Alec and Mora Dickson sent eight young men on volunteer missions overseas, VSO has placed over 42,000 volunteers in more than 140 countries in Africa, Asia, the Pacific, the Caribbean, Eastern Europe, and Latin America. Today, it recruits volunteers from around the world through local offices in Canada, Kenya, the Netherlands, the Philippines, India, and Ireland. Placements can last anywhere from 2 weeks to 6 months.

VSO programs are centered around development and cooperation in six different areas: HIV/AIDS, education, health and social well-being, disability, participation and governance, and livelihood security. The average age of a VSO volunteer is 41, meaning that participants bring the wealth of experience and skills of mature adults to the communities where they work. Volunteers are placed according to their education and skills. VSO looks for people with expertise in business, communications, community development, education, engineering and technical trades, health, HIV/AIDS, and natural resources. VSO also organizes national volunteering, in which partners are placed in communities within their own country.

*"Every day people thank us... not for doing the work for them, but for giving them the opportunity to work themselves. But it goes both ways. I'm incredibly grateful for the chance to share my skills here and to learn."*
*—Volunteer Stephanie Stoker*

| | |
|---|---|
| Past accomplishments | 7/10 |
| International reach | 4/10 |
| Tangibility | 7.5/10 |
| Peace and hope | 7/10 |
| Building a better world | 4/10 |
| Average score | 5.9/10 |

**Left:** Volunteers planting rice in a paddy field in Chittagong.

International adoption, or intercountry adoption, involves becoming the legal and permanent parents of a child born in another country. Each country establishes its own rules and regulations for international adoption. Generally, however, prospective parents must meet the legal adoption requirements of their country of residence and those of the country in which the child was born.

In the early 1990s, the organization called The Hague Conference on Private International Law (HCPIL) recognized that corruption and exploitation can arise from international adoption. It was obvious that some form of legal protection was required for adoptive parents and, especially, for children. The Convention on the Protection of Children and Cooperation in Respect of Intercountry Adoption was developed by the HCPIL in 1993; and as of 2008, seventy-six countries had ratified it. Some countries, such as the United Arab Emirates, forbid international adoption and others, such as China and Vietnam, have well-established adoption laws. Some African nations have laws requiring potential parents to have extended residency, which can make it difficult to proceed with adoption plans.

**Above:** The Hague Bureau has 69 member states, which have to respect the Hague Conference.

The Hague Convention requires that governments from the child's birth country and the child's potential future home agree to the adoption. The child must be under age 16, be unmarried, and live in a country that adheres to the Convention. It is also vital that the child's birth parents or legal guardian give irrevocable consent and proof of relationship to the child is required. The Convention does not assist in individual adoptions; rather, its mandate is administrative and protective in broad legal issues such as ensuring measures are in place to protect potential adoptees, standardizing the processes between countries, and preventing child abuse such as trafficking.

*"Intercountry adoptions shall be made in the best interests of the child."*
*—The Hague Convention*

| | |
|---|---|
| Past accomplishments | 6/10 |
| International reach | 7/10 |
| Tangibility | 5/10 |
| Peace and hope | 4.5/10 |
| Building a better world | 7/10 |
| Average score | 5.9/10 |

*Patrick Bonneville: One way to achieve peace and neighborliness is to share and understand values, differences, and heritage. One special agency from the United Nations has the mandate to bring peace by promoting culture, science, and education. The organization is known as UNESCO, which stands for United Nations Educational, Scientific and Cultural Organization. UNESCO has been criticized for being bureaucracy-heavy, but the organization has succeeded in restructuring itself in the past few years in order to become more efficient.*

UNESCO was created on November 16, 1945, to "contribute to peace and security by promoting international collaboration through education, science, and culture in order to further universal respect for justice, the rule of law, and the human rights and fundamental freedoms proclaimed in the UN Charter."

Its hefty budget of $631 million funds missions concerning education, freedom of the press and media, historical concerns, and even cultural and environmental protection. UNESCO is responsible for the World Heritage program, which catalogues, names, and conserves cultural or natural sites for posterity. The organization is also behind the Seville Statement on Violence, which was adopted in 1989. The Seville Statement refutes "the notion that organized human violence is biologically determined." The statement concludes: "Just as 'wars begin in the minds of men,' peace also begins in our minds. The same species who invented war is capable of inventing peace. The responsibility lies with each of us."

UNESCO initiated the Programme on Man and the Biosphere, whose mission is to share knowledge that will help prevent biodiversity loss and reinforce environment sustainability. Today, the program protects over 500 reserves in more than 105 countries, including the Central Amazon in Brazil, the Charlevoix in Canada, Wuyishan in China, and the Olympic National Park in the United States.

UNESCO has a program specifically designed to encourage creativity and another to collect and preserve international "memories," or cultural artifacts. These items include the Declaration of the Rights of Man and of the Citizen, the literary estate of Goethe, the archives of the Dutch East India Company, Nicolaus Copernicus' written masterpiece *De Revolutionibus Orbium Coelest,* and the 1939 American classic movie *The Wizard of Oz.*

**Left:** World Heritage program and UNESCO logos.

| | |
|---|---|
| Past accomplishments | 7/10 |
| International reach | 9/10 |
| Tangibility | 4/10 |
| Peace and hope | 4/10 |
| Building a better world | 5/10 |
| Average score | 5.8/10 |

There are several success stories in the world of grassroots organizations. When one of them can count over two million members and supporters, it can count itself among the best. Friends of the Earth International (FOEI) is one such organization. FOEI is in fact a network of environmental groups from around the world that works within communities to include the people who live there.

**Above:** Friends of the Earth's International secretariat is based in amsterdam.

The network was formed in 1971 with the marriage of four other organizations from France, Sweden, England, and the United States. Today, seventy-seven associations work together as FOEI on issues ranging from nuclear energy to whaling. Its vision is powerful: peace and sustainability in a world where all people live in harmony with their environment and with each other. Collectively, it moves toward creating that world by working with indigenous peoples, farmers' movements, trade unions, human rights groups, and other associations to deal with environmental injustices, human rights issues, and sustainability.

Partner organizations must meet a number of FOEI criteria in order to join the network. They must be independent from political parties, economic interests, and state, religious, and ethnic organizations; work at both the national and the grassroots levels; work on the main environmental issues in their countries, as opposed to working as a single-issue group; participate in international campaigns of FOEI whenever relevant; have open and democratic structures and be non-sexist; consider environmental issues in their social, political, and human rights contexts; work as a pressure group, as much as possible, within the national context; campaign, educate, and do research; and maximize cooperation with other organizations.

*"We believe that we can stop the current global environmental and social crisis, and that we can contribute to a transformation towards a better world."*
—*Friends of the Earth*

| | |
|---|---|
| Past accomplishments | 5/10 |
| International reach | 8/10 |
| Tangibility | 4/10 |
| Peace and hope | 6/10 |
| Building a better world | 6/10 |
| Average score | 5.8/10 |

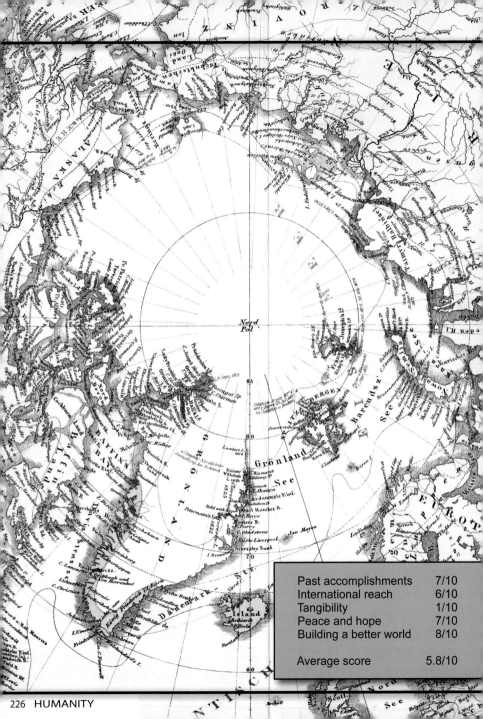

| | |
|---|---|
| Past accomplishments | 7/10 |
| International reach | 6/10 |
| Tangibility | 1/10 |
| Peace and hope | 7/10 |
| Building a better world | 8/10 |
| | |
| Average score | 5.8/10 |

*Patrick Bonneville: Since the melting of the polar ice cap was first recorded, the Arctic has become a source of potential dispute between Northern countries, especially between Canada, the United States, Russia, and Denmark (Greenland). They all want a piece of that "melting ice," or rather what's hiding underneath the ice.*

In 1996, the Ottawa Declaration formally established the Arctic Council, composed of member states that border or have territories in the Arctic region. The Council is a high-level government organization that deliberates on issues related to Arctic territories and their indigenous peoples.

An enormous geographical region of more than 30 million square kilometres and spanning twenty-four time zones, the international Arctic region is home to about four million people, thirty different indigenous peoples, and countless native languages. It is rich in natural resources, and compared to other parts of our planet, it is relatively clean.

**Left:** Arctic Ocean map, most territories belonging to Canada and Russia.
**Above:** Icebreaker driving through ice floe.

Member states are: Canada, the United States, Russia, Denmark, Finland, Iceland, Norway, and Sweden. Observer states are China, Japan, South Korea, the European Union, as well as specific representation from France, Netherlands, Germany, Italy, Poland, and Spain.

The Arctic Council also has non-country members who enjoy permanent participation and are generally from indigenous communities. They are: the Aleut International Association; the Arctic Athabaskan Council; the Gwich'in Council International; the Inuit Circumpolar Council; the Saami Council; Russian Arctic Indigenous Peoples of the North; and the Arctic Council Chairmanship. Its purpose is simple: to ensure full participation with regard to Council projects. Indeed, an important facet of the council is protecting the Arctic's indigenous communities with regard to development within the territories, particularly with issues concerning sustainable development and environmental protection.

The Arctic Council has developed six working groups that study issues affecting the Arctic: the Arctic Contaminants Action Program; Arctic Monitoring and Assessment Program; Conservation of Arctic Flora and Fauna; Emergency Prevention, Preparedness and Response; Protection of the Arctic Marine Environment; and the Sustainable Development Working Group. Arctic Council programs and action plans are centered around Arctic and circumpolar biodiversity monitoring, climate impact, and human development.

The International Council on Monuments and Sites (ICOMOS) is a non-governmental organization of professionals dedicated to the conservation of architecture and archaeological heritage. Its more than 9,500 members are landscape architects, architects, archaeologists, town planners, engineers, experts in artifact conservation, heritage administrators, art historians, and art archivists. ICOMOS is an important advisor to UNESCO on World Heritage Sites.

The history of ICOMOS can be traced back to Athens, Greece, in 1931, when a conference was held about historic building preservation and restoration. Organized by the International Museum, the findings of the conference led to the Athens Charter, which proposed guidelines for organizing international and national cultural conservation initiatives. In 1965, after the devastating effects of two world wars on humanity's architectural heritage, ICOMOS was founded.

ICOMOS is composed of a secretariat, a documentation center, national committees, and international scientific committees. The secretariat organizes forums where professionals can exchange ideas and collect and analyze information related to conservation. ICOMOS also joins forces with national and international organizations to create access to information and documents. The protection of our cultural property is supported through other ICOMOS initiatives. The Heritage at Risk program, endorsed by members in 1999, seeks to identify threatened places, monuments, and sites that have cultural value to humanity. The program examines, identifies, and publishes reports on sites that are in a fragile and vulnerable state. The reports also explain the country's government processes, the obstacles to protection, and possible solutions. The reports also present case studies that can add to the insight gained from success stories.

| | |
|---|---|
| Past accomplishments | 7/10 |
| International reach | 8.5/10 |
| Tangibility | 2.5/10 |
| Peace and hope | 6/10 |
| Building a better world | 4/10 |
| | |
| Average score | 5.6/10 |

**Left:** Building in Old Havana, repairs monitored by ICOMOS.

Horrified by events during and after the Franco-Prussian War of 1870-71, a group of Belgian lawyers came together in 1873 to create an organization that would contribute to the development of international law. The Institute of International Law (IIL) would be independent of government influence—essential for its goal of addressing the lack of compliance to international agreements that appeared widespread.

Gustave Moynier (also a founding member of the International Committee of the Red Cross) and other founders were some of the most respected lawyers of the day. Their purpose was to advance the progress of international law rather than manage legal issues. Today, the IIL is an organization that studies and researches law agreements worldwide, working to bring positive developments about in international law. The Institute generally meets once every two years with an agenda to review legal developments and examine recent studies. They adopt resolutions and present them to national governments and international organizations. These motions are also presented to the scientific community with the hope of obtaining support for the soundness of the projects.

**Above:** The institute has respected members from all over the world, including judges of the International Criminal Court.

The most important element of this organization is its mandate to peaceably advance negotiations and arbitrition between states in the course of legal decisions that might otherwise be contentious. For its efforts, the Institute of International Law was granted the Nobel Peace Prize in 1904.

*"Every State and every non-State entity participating in an armed conflict are legally bound vis-à-vis each other as well as all other members of the international community to respect international humanitarian law in all circumstances, and any other State is legally entitled to demand respect for this body of law. No State or non-State entity can escape its obligations by denying the existence of an armed conflict."*
*—The Institute of International Law, Session of Berlin - 1999*

| | |
|---|---|
| Past accomplishments | 7/10 |
| International reach | 7/10 |
| Tangibility | 3/10 |
| Peace and hope | 6/10 |
| Building a better world | 5/10 |
| Average score | 5.6/10 |

An early version of the Union of South American Nations—known by its Spanish acronym, UNASUR—was created in May 2008 on the model of the European Union. Its purpose is to unite the countries of South America in trade and commerce with the goal of becoming an international economical force. Despite its promising mandate, the organization has yet to be ratified by the ninth South American state required for legitimacy. The union must also effectively overcome internal differences if it is to be successful in its goals of a single parliament, currency, and passport as well as in defence matters, immigration, and economic development.

UNASUR proposes to: create a single market in South America by 2019; create an interoceanic highway that will better connect the Pacific Ocean nations with the rest of the continent; introduce important telecommunications, maritime, and energy initiatives; facilitate interstate travel by requiring only the presentation of an identity card for stays in other member states of under ninety days; and advance the scientific and technological development of member states through funding from the new Bank of the South, based upon the World Bank. The union also proposes to utilize the Bank to promote projects that equalize investment throughout South America.

*"If my death contributes to the ceasing of the parties and to the consolidation of the union, I shall go down in peace to my tomb."*
*—Simon Bolivar*

| | |
|---|---|
| Past accomplishments | 7/10 |
| International reach | 4/10 |
| Tangibility | 4/10 |
| Peace and hope | 7/10 |
| Building a better world | 5/10 |
| Average score | 5.4/10 |

**Below:** South American presidents during the third Summit of Heads of State of the Union of South American Nations, Brasília, 2008.
**Right:** Map of South America.

*"The oceans are dying in our lifetime and it's not for want of laws and regulations. The problem is enforcement. Governments are not enforcing the laws, so we have to"*
—*Paul Watson, founder of the Sea Shepherd Conservation Society*

*Patrick Bonneville: They do what they have to do. I am a fan.*

In 1981, ex-Greenpeace member Paul Watson founded his non-governmental agency, the Sea Shepherd Conservation Society (SSCS). It had been operating since 1977 under the name Earth Force Society. Watson convinced the head of the British Fund for Animals to fund his first vessel, the Sea Shepherd. From its earliest days, the SSCS has been concerned with the health and protection of oceans, specifically the whaling, fishing, and seal hunting industries.

Although supported by many important figures, including the Dalai Lama, several governments and organizations have criticized Sea Shepherd as "rogue" rescuers, often referring to them as pirates; some have gone as far as to call them terrorists.

The reference is understandable: Watson believes strongly in a very physical approach to protection. His tactics include disabling whaling vessels at harbor, disrupting the seal hunts in Canada, purposely colliding with other ships, and shooting laser lights in an

**Previous page:** Japanese whalers collide with the Ady Gil.
**Left:** Encounter in the Arctic Ocean.
**Below:** Crew members are hosed by water cannons from Japanese harpoon whaling ship.
**Right:** The ship Steve Irwin in Hobart.

effort to disorient whalers, among other things. More recently, in February 2010, pro-whaling activists led a protest against the group in Australia. They accused the SSCS of practicing "absolutely racial discrimination against Japanese people." Australia demanded a guarantee of "good character" from Watson and First Officer Peter Hammarstedt before it would provide them business visas. The men were compelled to provide police references from the United States, Canada, and Norway.

Sea Shepherd's mission is to assume a law enforcement role under the United Nations World Charter for Nature. This charter was adopted by the United Nations General Assembly on November 9, 1982. Today, the SSCS relies greatly on the media to get its message across. Fund-raising efforts are kept to a minimum, leaving the organization to rely on the Internet, grants, advertising sales, and donations.

| Past accomplishments | 4/10 |
| International reach | 5.5/10 |
| Tangibility | 4/10 |
| Peace and hope | 7/10 |
| Building a better world | 6.5/10 |
| | |
| Average score | 5.4/10 |

*"Everybody needs beauty as well as bread, places to play in and pray in, where nature may heal and give strength to body and soul alike."*
*-John Muir, on the Yosemite, 1912*

The Sierra Club was founded in 1892, in San Francisco, California. As the oldest and largest environmental organization in the United States, it has grown to include hundreds of thousands of members throughout the U.S.A. and is affiliated with the Sierra Club in Canada. The group is active in the protection of communities, wild places, and environmental concerns in the United States and around the world.

Conservationist John Muir founded the Sierra Club and served as its first president. John Muir might be considered a man ahead of his time. Born in Scotland and relocated to the United States, he dedicated his life to educating people about and promoting wild spaces and species. His efforts led to the creation of a number of national parks, including Yosemite, Sequoia, Mount Rainier, Petrified Forest, and Grand Canyon. His legacy also includes his image on the back of the American twenty-five cent coin.

Most of the Sierra Club's 500 staff work at the organization's headquarters in San Francisco, California. Others lobby policy makers in Washington, DC. General members of the club belong to state-wide chapters in the U.S.A., or to national chapters in other countries. At every level, the Sierra Club works to find solutions for conservation issues affecting our planet: agriculture, biotechnology,

**Left:** Muir Woods National Monument, California.
**Above:** John Muir, founder of the Sierra Club, was featured on two U.S. commemorative postage stamps.

energy, environmental justice, forest and wilderness management, global issues, land management, military issues, nuclear issues, oceans, pollution and waste management, transportation, urban and land use policies, water resources, and wildlife conservation.

Today, almost one hundred years after Muir's death, the Sierra Club remains an essential feature of the conservation landscape in the U.S.A. and beyond.

People for the Ethical Treatment of Animals (PETA) is the world's largest animal rights advocacy organization. It has more than two million members and supporters who decry the way animals are used in factory farms, laboratories, the entertainment industry, fashion, or in any other way that jeopardizes their well-being. PETA's principal message is that animals deserve the same respect as humans and are not ours to use as we see fit.

Founded in 1980 and headquartered in Norfolk, Virginia, PETA's mandate is to conduct public education, cruelty investigations, research, animal rescues, special events, and protest campaigns. They also lobby for changes in legislation and use media pressure in their goal to eradicate the use of animals in sports such as racing, cock-fighting, bull-fighting, and fishing.

PETA's efforts have led to several notable successes: in 1981, in the Silver Spring Monkey case, the organization successfully brought animal cruelty charges against a research scientist at a primate research laboratory. While the case was lost on appeal, it did lead to an amendment to the Animal Welfare Act in which researchers must not cause unnecessary suffering to laboratory animals. Effectively, this case launched PETA into the nationally and internationally recognized group it is today.

Other PETA campaigns have led to permanent bans on animal testing by several companies, including Benetton (the first to do so), AVON, Revlon, and Estée Lauder. PETA also successfully pressured McDonald's, Burger King, and other fast-food restaurants to introduce vegetarian options to their menus and recruited top fashion designers in a commitment to not use fur in their designs.

PETA's campaigns sometimes stirr up controversy, as they often rely on shocking or upsetting imagery and words to relay their messages. In a campaign to promote vegetarianism, for example, one poster portrays a 1950s-style mother butchering a terrified rabbit with the caption "Your Mother Kills Animals." In a somewhat lighter tone, the PETA "I'd Rather Go Naked Than Wear Fur" campaign recruited fashion supermodels to pose naked for posters and billboards seen by millions around the Western world. While PETA's strategies might be objectionable to some, there is little doubt that their convictions have led to improved conditions for pets, livestock, and wildlife.

**Above:** PETA members are arrested in Washington.
**Right:** PETA member protesting in front of the Ontario parliament.

| | |
|---|---|
| Past accomplishments | 4/10 |
| International reach | 3.5/10 |
| Tangibility | 5/10 |
| Peace and hope | 6/10 |
| Building a better world | 7.5/10 |
| | |
| Average score | 5.2/10 |

*Patrick Bonneville: Museums are the guardians of humanity's most important treasures. They play a vital role in our world as they display the best and the worst of what humanity has achieved so far. ICOM links museums together and helps them preserve this priceless heritage.*

The International Council of Museums (ICOM) is committed to the conservation of the world's natural and cultural heritage. It was created in 1946 as a non-profit, non-governmental network of museums and conservation experts who work alongside UNESCO in developing museums that conserve art, militaria, transportation, and ethnographic material. ICOM is affiliated with seventeen other international associations.

Based in Paris, France, the headquarters is the home of both the ICOM Secretariat and the UNESCO-ICOM Museum Information Centre. ICOM is financed primarily by membership fees and supported by various governments and other bodies. Members benefit from free or reduced entry to each others' museums.

**Left:** The Louvre is home to nearly 35,000 objects from prehistory to the 19th century.
**Above:** Interior of Great Hall in British Museum.

ICOM's 26,000 members from 139 countries participate in national and international activities that include workshops, publications, training, twinning programs, and the promotion of museums through International Museum Day—May 18. A strategic plan adopted by ICOM's General Assembly includes projects for the development of expertise for conservation professionals, raising awareness about museums, training personnel, and combating the illicit trafficking of cultural property. Notably, ICOM's regional Red Lists are an index of cultural heritage items at risk of being looted from archaeological sites or stolen from museums.

| | |
|---|---|
| Past accomplishments | 7/10 |
| International reach | 8/10 |
| Tangibility | 3/10 |
| Peace and hope | 5/10 |
| Building a better world | 3/10 |
| Average score | 5.2/10 |

*"Museums enable people to explore collections for inspiration, learning and enjoyment. They are institutions that collect, safeguard and make accessible artifacts and specimens, which they hold in trust for society."*
—The UK Museums Association

**Left:** The eighth Asian Cooperation Dialogue Ministerial Meeting held in Colombo, 2009.

Forty-seven countries make up Asia as we know it; they are home to about 60 percent of the world's population. From distant history through to modern times, a number of these countries have been at war with each other. The Asia Cooperation Dialogue (ACD) hopes to introduce a new chapter to this history—one of cooperation and trust. This forum for discussion was established in June 2002 in Cha-Am, Thailand. It groups together the leaders of eighteen Asian nations in order to develop strategies that will unite the continent's strengths and economic potential. It also aims to fortify relations within the continent.

The ACD focuses on two dimensions: dialogue and projects. At annual meetings, members discuss matters of cooperation and unity. ACD foreign ministers also meet during the UN's fall General Assembly to exchange updates on issues of concern, especially that of strengthening Asia's position in the international arena. ACD projects are centered around cooperation on matters involving agriculture, energy, biotechnology, tourism, poverty alleviation, IT development, e-education, and financial cooperation.

At the community level, the ACD hosts think-tank symposiums that are made up of academic institutions, development networks, and research groups nominated by member countries to serve as the analytical branch of ACD. The think-tanks are mandated to study and support the development of the association and support its major projects.

The Asian countries who are not yet members of ACD have all expressed an intention of eventual membership. They are Afghanistan, Armenia, Azerbaijan, Cyprus, Egypt, Georgia, Iraq, Israel, Jordan, Lebanon, Maldives, Nepal, North Korea, Syria, Timor-Leste, Turkey, Turkmenistan, and Yemen.

*"We must learn to trust, confide and work together for our mutual benefits, not viewing one another as competitors, but rather as partners and allies."*
*—Thailand's Prime Minister Thaksin Shinawatra, June 2002*

| | |
|---|---|
| Past accomplishments | 2/10 |
| International reach | 7/10 |
| Tangibility | 4/10 |
| Peace and hope | 5/10 |
| Building a better world | 8/10 |
| | |
| Average score | 5.2/10 |

ProLiteracy Worldwide is a non-profit organization that helps people around the world learn how to read. It was founded in 2002 in Syracuse, New York, when two literacy organizations merged in purpose and administration. Laubach Literacy International and Literacy Volunteers of America, Inc. merged to form ProLiteracy Worldwide to bring reading, writing, math, and computing skills to people around the world, in their own languages.

In the United States, the organization accompanies people in their goal to learn how to read, write, do math, and prepare for General Equivalency Diplomas so that they may find sustainable work and raise their self-esteem. Abroad, ProLiteracy is active in fifty countries, bringing literacy to people in their own languages through local partners. These partnerships also embrace other objectives, such as generating income, preserving the environment, addressing local health concerns, promoting peace and conflict resolution, and fostering education opportunities for adults and children. The organization is also a national and international advocate for literacy, including lobbying governmental representatives to support adult education.

According to ProLiteracy Worldwide, more than 776 million adults around the world cannot read or write in their mother tongue; two-thirds of them are women. Literacy is a tool that can lead a nation toward education and self-sufficiency. The founder of Laubach Literacy International, Dr. Frank C. Laubach, saw a direct connection between literacy and poverty. He developed a one-on-one program, "Each One Teach One"; where resources to improve literacy, and ultimately eradicate poverty, are found within villages themselves. If each person who could read and write taught another, the disadvantages of illiteracy could be reduced.

Interestingly, the highest literacy rates in the world are found in Poland, Cuba, Estonia, Barbados, Latvia, and Slovenia. The lowest, out of 177 countries, are Guinea, Niger, Chad, Mali, and Burkina Faso.

*"The greatest gift that we could give, the greatest legacy that we could leave, would be for every child in every country to have the chance that 75 million children still do not have today—the chance to go to school, to spell their name, to count their age, and perhaps to learn of the generation that is fighting to make their freedom real."*
*—UK Prime Minister Gordon Brown*

| | |
|---|---|
| Past accomplishments | 5/10 |
| International reach | 6/10 |
| Tangibility | 4/10 |
| Peace and hope | 7/10 |
| Building a better world | 3/10 |
| Average score | 5.0/10 |

Established in July 2002, the African Union is an intergovernmental union of fifty-three African states whose goal is to unite in the face of Africa's challenges and increase the volume of the African voice. The issues the AU must deal with are daunting: AIDS/HIV, malaria, non-democratic regimes, civil wars, economic issues, poverty, education, ecological sustainability, the standard of living, and famine.

The combined states of the African Union constitute the world's seventeenth-largest economy with a nominal GDP of $500 billion, ranking after the Netherlands. By measuring GDP by purchasing power parity (PPP), the Union's economy totals $1.515 trillion, putting it in eleventh place, after Brazil. At the same time, they have a combined total debt of $200 billion.

The precursor to the AU was the Organization of African Unity (OAU), whose objectives were to eliminate apartheid and the negative traces of colonization. Modeled on the United Nations, the OAU was geared toward unity, solidarity, and cooperation for economic and social development. As global markets changed, however, and the European Union was formed, the inspiration for a new sort of collective had arrived.

In September 1999, the heads of state and governments of the OAU signed the Sirte Declaration that called for the establishment of an African Union. The goal was to create a comprehensive association charged with the task of bringing Africa into the global economy while addressing the serious negative aspects affecting African life. The AU has a determined vision for the African people—to bring together countries and create an atmosphere of peace, security, and stability.

The Union currently has three suspended members; Mauritania (suspended after the coup d'état of 2008), Guinea (suspended after the coup d'état of 2008) and Madagascar (suspended after the 2009 Malagasy political crisis). Morocco left the OAU in 1984 and has not indicated any intention to become part of the African Union.

Several other countries are currently involved in situations that are considered controversial or difficult for the African Union to carry. These countries are experiencing civil war or political crises that complicate their economy and endanger civilians. Other countries are burdened by health and environmental issues.

| Past accomplishments | 5/10 |
| International reach | 4/10 |
| Tangibility | 5/10 |
| Peace and hope | 7/10 |
| Building a better world | 4/10 |
| | |
| Average score | 5.0/10 |

**Right:** Flag of the African Union.

*Kimberly Murray: In order to bring about positive change in our world, we must instill in our children the idea that peace is an option.*

In 1993, American journalist John Wallach attended a state dinner with politicians from Israel, Egypt, and the Palestinian Authority. At the event, he invited each representative to send fifteen young people from their respective countries to a new camp he founded. With three American kids, the group of forty-eight gathered in the state of Maine, in the United States, and participated in the first Seeds of Peace camp. The campers then traveled to witness the signing of the Declaration of Principles (Oslo Accords) in Washington DC.

Since then, over 4,000 kids from several conflict zones have "graduated" from the camp. Seeds of Peace has welcomed children from Jordan, Afghanistan, India, Pakistan, Cyprus, and the Balkans. There are now offices in Haifa, Tel Aviv, Ramallah, Cairo, and Amman, where camp graduates are able to participate in discussion forums.

The campers are guided and mentored with emotional support, respect, and empathy to ensure that the psychological effects of the program are well assimilated. They also participate in regular camp activitites, such as sports and cultural and artistic programs. They share rooms with the neighbors they have been raised to hate and with whom they learn tolerance and comprehension. During the three-week camp, the youth experience a deprogramming of sorts and they begin to see that peace is possible.

Seeds of Peace campers walk away from the peace and security of the camp to return to their conflict-burdened homelands. Having spent time amongst their "enemies," however, discussing their issues, and sharing their values, fears, and hatred, their attitudes typically have evolved during their experience at the camp.

These young campers will become the leaders of tomorrow. Seeds of Peace endows them with the skills needed to be leaders in reconciliation and tolerance. These kids, from some of the most war-torn regions of our planet, have learned that confidence in the peace process is possible and crucial.

**Above:** Bonding in a Seeds of Peace camp.
**Right:** Building a world without boundaries.

| | |
|---|---|
| Past accomplishments | 2.5/10 |
| International reach | 2/10 |
| Tangibility | 5/10 |
| Peace and hope | 8/10 |
| Building a better world | 7/10 |
| Average score | 4.9/10 |

*Patrick Bonneville: The world belongs to our children. Let them take the stage. Let them inspire us all.*

**Left:** Encouraging youth to build a better world by getting involved.

Do Something believes that teenagers really can do something—they can make an important difference in the world. Do Something is an American NGO that aims to inspire, support, and celebrate this unique demographic making them advocates for such causes as the environment, health and fitness, HIV and sexuality, animal welfare, international human rights, poverty, discrimination, disaster relief, bullying, and many others. Do Something provides the support and resources needed to help young people put their thoughts into action.

Do Something was founded by actor Andrew Shue in 1993. He purportedly wanted to help teens discover that community activism was as essential to a healthy lifestyle as sports and cultural activities. Currently, only 23 percent of teenagers are active volunteers in their communities; Do Something aims to spark the imagination of young people so that eventually more than half of teenagers will become actively involved in their communities or in the global community.

Headquartered today in New York City, the organization uses primarily the Internet, TV, and pop culture to reach its target population. Its programs provide a framework for planning, coordinating, budgeting, administering, directing, recruiting, executing, and finishing a project. The Do Something Awards endow prize money of up to $100,000 for a young person's organization or cause. Now that's doing something!

*"DoSomething.org is a very special part of my life now. It has not only given me new hopes and dreams to create a significant difference in the world but also that it is POSSIBLE to create a difference being only one person."*
*—Radhika, Do Something's Youth Advisory Council*

| | |
|---|---|
| Past accomplishments | 3/10 |
| International reach | 3/10 |
| Tangibility | 6/10 |
| Peace and hope | 7/10 |
| Building a better world | 5/10 |
| Average score | 4.8/10 |

*"Twenty years from now you will be more disappointed by the things you didn't do than by the ones you did do. So throw off the bowlines, sail away from the safe harbor. Catch the trade winds in your sails. Explore. Dream. Discover."*
-Mark Twain

*Patrick Bonneville: Youth hostels are like a door to humanity. There is no better school than travel.*

Hostelling International (HI) is a group of more than ninety youth hostel associations in over eighty countries worldwide; it represents some 4,500 youth hostels. HI implements high international quality standards to ensure that the traveler's stay at a hostel is comfortable and fun.

The international hostel movement was born in 1909, when German schoolteacher Richard Schirrmann took some students on a field trip. A fan of teaching from directly within the environment, on this particular excursion, the group was caught in a thunderstorm.

They were lucky to find accommodations in a schoolhouse where they were given straw to make beds and milk from a local farmer. In Schirrmann's mind, a brilliant idea was forming:

*"The schools in Germany could very well be used to provide accommodation during the holidays. Villages could have a friendly youth hostel, situated a day's walk from each other, to welcome young hikers . . . Two classrooms will suffice, one for boys and one for girls."*

The idea caught on and in 1912, the first true hostel opened in the old castle of Altena. Two rooms were fitted with triple-tier bunk beds, and a common kitchen and separate bathrooms completed the transformation. The original rooms are still on display today.

Indeed, hostelling has become more sophisticated with time but still retains its initial purpose: to offer clean, friendly, inexpensive beds for travelers on a budget. Initially, hostels were intended to house young people, generally between eighteen and thirty years of age. Today, however, many hostels accept families and senior travellers as well. Hostelling International is a non-profit organization that is driven by its membership.

| | |
|---|---|
| Past accomplishments | 4/10 |
| International reach | 9.5/10 |
| Tangibility | 3/10 |
| Peace and hope | 2.5/10 |
| Building a better world | 5/10 |
| Average score | 4.8/10 |

**Left:** Huwaida Arraf of the Free Gaza movement. She is a Palestinian-American, and an Israeli citizen.
**Right:** Free Gaza ship getting close to Gaza shore.

*Patrick Bonneville: It takes courage to get aboard a small yacht stacked with emergency supplies and go in the direction of Gaza, where one will be under attack from the powerful Israeli army. It takes a lot of courage to face the Israeli fleet on the Mediteranean Sea with public opinion as the only weapon onboard.*

At the Gaza Strip, nobody gets in and nobody gets out. There has been much struggle, death, and anguish about and for this small piece of land. Free Gaza is a movement to get help to those who need it in Gaza. It is based on the principles of two great peace leaders: Ghandi and Martin Luther King. The Free Gaza organization undertook a simple but dangerous mission: buy a boat and sail it to Gaza to deliver aid, in defiance of the Israeli siege. On August 5, 2008, they sailed to Gaza.

The Gaza Strip is an area of about 360 square kilometers of coastland along the Mediterranean Sea. It is home to about 1.5 million Palestinian residents and is, internally, under Palestinian Hamas control. Egypt governed Gaza from 1948 to 1967, after the Ottoman Empire and then the British Mandate of Palestine passed it into Israel's hands. Israel governed Gaza from 1967 to 2005. Although under Palestine control within its borders, Israel maintains military control of the Gaza airspace, land borders, and territorial waters.

Since 2000, hundreds of humanitarian workers from organizations around the world have been denied access to the Occupied Palestinian Territories by Israeli authorities. This has led to a humanitarian crisis, and the figures for unemployment, poverty, and childhood malnutrition are shocking. Free Gaza founders Bella Bocke, Eliza Ernshire, Greta Berlin, Mary Hughes, and Paul Larudee aimed to alleviate this crisis in an ingenious way. Their Free Gaza initiative has completed several successful missions to the area, where they have been able to bear witness to the violence imposed against the Palestinian people.

Free Gaza aims to raise awareness in the international community about the plight of Gaza's citizens and asks governments to review their policies regarding the Israeli occupation. Free Gaza, in its essence, embodies the simplest of humanitarian principles: respect the human rights of everyone, regardless of race, tribe, religion, ethnicity, nationality, citizenship, or language.

"We cannot just sit by and wait for Israel to decide to stop the killing. When states and the international bodies responsible for taking action to stop such atrocities choose to be impotent, then we—the citizens of the world—must act. Our common humanity demands nothing less."
—Huwaida Arraf, founder of the International Solidarity Movement (ISM) and member of Free Gaza

| | |
|---|---|
| Past accomplishments | 5/10 |
| International reach | 2.5/10 |
| Tangibility | 5/10 |
| Peace and hope | 7/10 |
| Building a better world | 4/10 |
| | |
| Average score | 4.7/10 |

# PHOTO CREDITS

The following abbreviations are used:

b = background
l = left
r = right
u = upper

| | |
|---|---|
| 4 | Philip Lange/Dreamstime.com |
| 6 | Oleksandr Batsyn/Dreamstime.com |
| 10 b | UN Photo/John Isaac |
| 12 | Erickn/Dreamstime.com |
| 14 | UN Photo/KB |
| 14 | Oleksandr Batsyn/Dreamstime.com |
| 14 b | Oleksandr Batsyn/Dreamstime.com |
| 15 | UN Photo/Stuart Price |
| 16 | UN Photo/Marco Dormino |
| 16 | Oleksandr Batsyn/Dreamstime.com |
| 16 b | Oleksandr Batsyn/Dreamstime.com |
| 17 | UN Photo/Marco Dormino |
| 17 | UN Photo/Evan Schneider |
| 18 b | Joseph Moran/Dreamstime.com |
| 18 | UN Photo/Stuart Price |
| 19 | UN Photo/Evan Schneider |
| 20 b | UN Photo/Evan Schneider |
| 20 | UN Photo/Evan Schneider |
| 21 | UN Photo/Marie Frechon |
| 22 | American Red Cross/Dennis Drenner |
| 24 | American Red Cross |
| 24 b | ICRC |
| 25 | American Red Cross/Talia Frankel |
| 26 | American Red Cross |
| 27 b | ICRC |
| 27 l | IFRC/Eric Quintero |
| 27 r | American Red Cross/Talia Frenkel |
| 28 | American Red Cross/Talia Frenkel |
| 29 | ICRC |
| 30 | UNICEF/Thierry Delvigne-Jean |
| 32 b | Andrea Presazzi/Dreamstime.com |
| 32 | UNICEF/Marta Ramoneda |
| 33 l | UNICEF |
| 34 | UNICEF/Chulho Hyun |
| 35 r | David McKenzie/UNICEF |
| 35 b | Sportgraphic/Dreamstime.com |
| 35 l | UNICEF/Josh Este |
| 36 | MSF Canada |
| 38 | MSF Canada |
| 39 | Nicky Cohen de Lara-Kroon |
| 40 | Dgrilla/Dreamstime.com |
| 41 b | Samc3352/Dreamstime.com |
| 41 r | World Economic Forum |
| 42 | Jeppo75/Dreamstime.com |
| 44 b | World Wide Fund for Nature |
| 45 | Ricardo Esplana Babor/Dreamstime.com |
| 46 | UNHCR/B. Bannon |
| 48 | UN Photo/Fred Noy |
| 49 l | UN Photo/Logan Abassi |
| 49 r | UN Photo/Logan Abassi |
| 50 l | UN Photo/Logan Abassi |
| 50 r | UN Photo/Logan Abassi |
| 50 b | World Food Programme |
| 51 | Suzanne Tucker/Dreamstime.com |
| 52 | Photowitch/Dreamstime.com |
| 54 | Pres Panayotov/Shutterstock |
| 55 b | Amnesty International |
| 55 r | Amnesty International |
| 56 b | Photowitch/Dreamstime.com |
| 56 l | STAND |
| 56 b | Amnesty International |
| 57 | Amnesty International |
| 58 b | WHO |
| 58 | WHO/Marko Kokic |
| 59 | Dreamshot/Dreamstime.com |
| 60 | UN Photo/Eskinder Debebe |
| 61 ur | WHO |
| 61 | UN Photo/x |
| 62 | Marcus Bleasdale/VII |
| 64 b | Michael Mayzel/Human Rights Watch |
| 64 ul | Human Rights Watch |
| 65 | Human Rights Watch |
| 66 | UNHCR/B.Heger |
| 68 l | UNHCR/P. Wiggers |
| 68 b | UN Photo/UNHCR |

| | | | |
|---|---|---|---|
| 69 | World Economic Forum/Remy Steinegger | 104 b | Rolffimages/Dreamstime.com |
| 70 | UN Photo/Evan Schneider | 104 | United Nations |
| 71 l | UNHCR/E. Denholm | 105 | Karuppasamy .g/Dreamstime.com |
| 71 r | UN Photo/Martine Perret | 106 | Picstudio/Dreamstime.com |
| 71 b | UNHCR/T.Irwin | 107 l | CARE-Archiv |
| 72 | US Mission Geneva | 107 r | CARE/Evelyn Hockstein |
| 73 | UN Photo/Yutaka Nagata | 108 | World Economic Forum |
| 74 | UN Photo/Fred Noy | 111 | Arun Bhargava/Dreamstime.com |
| 75 b | UN Photo/Fred Noy | 112 | Andrea Paggiaro/Dreamstime.com |
| 75 | FAO/Giulio Napolitano | 113 b | Stasys Eidiejus/dreamstime.com |
| 75 | FAO/Rocco Rorandelli | 114 | Salvation Army Canada |
| 76 | Save The Children | 114 b | Fabrizio Zanier/dreamstime.com |
| 78 | Nikhil Gangavane/Dreamstime.com | 115 | Salvation Army Canada |
| 78 | Save the Children España | 116 ur | World Vision UK |
| 79 | Save The Children | 116 lr | World Vision UK |
| 80 ur | International Labour Organization | 116 b | Gabe Palmer/Dreamstime.com |
| 80 lr | International Labour Organization | 117 | Martin Applegate/Dreamstime.com |
| 80 b | International Labour Organization | 118 | Presidencia de la Nación Argentina |
| 81 | International Labour Organization | 118 b | Markwaters/Dreamstime.com |
| 82 | Gösta Florman | 119 | Artefficient/Dreamstime.com |
| 82 b | Alfred Nobel | 120 b | Sebastian Kaulitzki/Shutterstock |
| 83 | Masr/Dreamstime.com | 121 | Cleo/Shutterstock |
| 84 | Armonn/Dreamstime.com | 122 b | UNEP |
| 86 | Tommy Schultz/dreamstime.com | 123 | Deanpictures/Dreamstime.com |
| 87 b | Peter Halasz | 124 | Mari Tefre/Global Crop Diversity Trust |
| 89 | British Nuclear Fuels PLC | 126 | Tyler Olson/Shutterstock |
| 90 | Oxfam New Zealand | 127 b | Global Crop Diversity Trust |
| 92 b | Oxfam America | 128 | Raul Vasquez/ORBIS International |
| 92 | Jane Ussher/Oxfam | 128 r | Arenacreative/Dreamstime.com |
| 93 | Oxfam America | 129 | Raul Vasquez/ORBIS International |
| 94 | ICJ | 129 | Orlando Florin Rosu/Dreamstime.com |
| 96 | Jan Kranendonk/Dreamstime.com | 130 b | War Child UK |
| 97 | Jeroen Bouman/Courtesy of the ICJ | 130 b | Evgene Gitlits/Dreamstime.com |
| 97 b | Jank1000/Dreamstime.com | 131 | Johanson09/Dreamstime.com |
| 98 | Zhang Lei/dreamstime.com | 132 | Icefields/Dreamstime.com |
| 100 b | Maksym Dragunov/dreamstime.com | 134 b | Ondacaracola/Dreamstime.com |
| 100 | Reporters Without Borders | 134 | Photograph from Bain News Service. |
| 101 | Reporters Without Borders | 134 | Linqong/Dreamstime.com |
| 102 | HFHI/Steffan Hacker | 135 | James Duhamel |
| 103 b | Habitat for Humanity International | 136 b | James Steidl/dreamstime.com |
| 103 | Emily Wong/unhabitat | 136 | US Department of Justice |

| | |
|---|---|
| 200 | NASA |
| 200 b | Vicspacewalker/dreamstime.com |
| 201 | Mike Brown/dreamstime.com |
| 202 b | PaulPaladin/Shutterstock |
| 202 | gary718/Shutterstock |
| 203 | Rose Waddell/Dreamstime.com |
| 204 | Lin Joe Yin/Dreamstime.com |
| 204 b | Dmitryp/dreamstime.com |
| 205 b | Sumnersgraphicsinc/Dreamstime.com |
| 205 | Gary Blakeley/Dreamstime.com |
| 206 | IBP |
| 206 b | IBP |
| 206 | Claus Mikosch/Dreamstime.com |
| 207 b | Dave Wetzel/Dreamstime.com |
| 207 | Fernando Soares/Dreamstime.com |
| 208 | Akhilesh Sharma/Dreamstime.com |
| 209 | Chee-onn Leong/Dreamstime.com |
| 210 b | The Nature Conservancy |
| 210 | The Nature Conservancy |
| 211 b | MMV |
| 211 | Petrafler/Dreamstime.com |
| 212 b | Ngo Thye Aun/Dreamstime.com |
| 212 l | Humane Society of the United States |
| 212 r | Humane Society of the United States |
| 213 | Ivan Tykhyi/Dreamstime.com |
| 214 | Hongqi Zhang/Dreamstime.com |
| 215 | Clearviewstock/Dreamstime.com |
| 215 b | Clearviewstock/Dreamstime.com |
| 216 | Worldwatch Institute |
| 217 b | Plan International |
| 217 | Plan España |
| 218 b | Gino Santa Maria/Dreamstime.com |
| 219 | ISO |
| 220 | Piers Brown |
| 221 | Varina and Jay Patel/Shutterstock |
| 221 b | Thomas M Perkins/Shutterstock |
| 222 | Sebastian Czapnik/Dreamstime.com |
| 223 | Jiri Castka/Dreamstime.com |
| 224 | Friends of the Earth |
| 225 | Darren Patterson/Dreamstime.com |
| 226 | Steven Wright/dreamstime.com |

| | |
|---|---|
| 227 | Achim Baqué/Dreamstime.com |
| 227 b | Ken Pilon/Dreamstime.com |
| 228 | Rgbspace/Dreamstime.com |
| 228 b | Roman Milert/Dreamstime.com |
| 229 | Tom Schmucker/Dreamstime.com |
| 230 | Agência Brasil |
| 230 b | Sourabh Jain/Dreamstime.com |
| 231 | Elena Elisseeva/Dreamstime.com |
| 232 | JoAnne McArthur/Sea Shepherd |
| 234 b | Sea Shepherd |
| 234 l | Sea Shepherd |
| 234 r | Sea Shepherd |
| 235 | Karen Graham/Dreamstime.com |
| 236 | William Perry/Dreamstime.com |
| 237 | Ken Brown/Shutterstock |
| 238 b | PETA |
| 238 | PETA |
| 239 | Sampete/Dreamstime.com |
| 240 | David Kovziridze/dreamstime.com |
| 241 | Marek Slusarczyk/dreamstime.com |
| 242 b | South Asian Foreign Relations |
| 242 | Ken Toh/Dreamstime.com |
| 243 | Ron Chapple Studios/Dreamstime.com |
| 244 | Dennis Owusu-ansah/Dreamstime.com |
| 245 | Amarcudic/Dreamstime.com |
| 246 b | Seeds of Peace |
| 246 | Seeds of Peace |
| 247 | Seeds of Peace |
| 248 b | Lomachevsky/Dreamstime.com |
| 248 | Michal Bednarek/Dreamstime.com |
| 249 | Roland Nagy/Dreamstime.com |
| 249 b | Raysie/Dreamstime.com |
| 250 b | Free Gaza |
| 250 | Free Gaza |
| 251 | Free Gaza |

*"An individual has not started living until he can rise above the narrow confines of his individualistic concerns to the broader concerns of all humanity."*
—*Martin Luther King, Jr.*